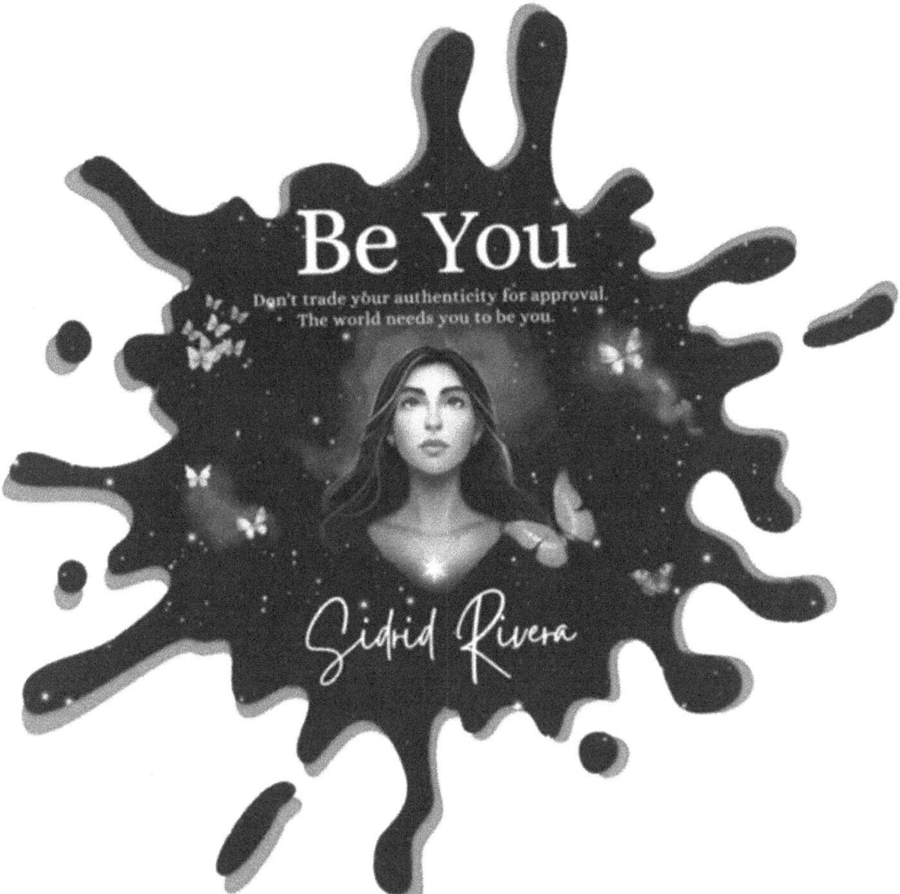
Be You
Don't trade your authenticity for approval.
The world needs you to be you.
Sidrid Rivera

Testimonials

" Sidrid Rivera and her company, Sidrid Rivera Enterprises, have played a powerful role in my life. If you're looking for a transformational life coach, I wholeheartedly recommend her. I've been coached by Sidrid in both my personal and business journey, and her guidance has helped me grow in ways I never imagined. I'm truly grateful to have her in my life and to now experience her wisdom through her powerful book, 'BE YOU.'

~ Haidee Lozano, Business Coaching Client

" Before working with Sidrid and reading her book 'BE YOU' I struggled deeply with feelings of unworthiness and believing I was truly loved. Through her step-by-step process, I began to break free from those limiting beliefs during our coaching sessions. The tools in this book are powerful—I was able to implement them in real time and experience transformation from the inside out. Today, I continue to walk in freedom, knowing that I am worthy—not because of what others say, but because I am God's masterpiece. That truth alone has changed everything for me.

~ Terri Schlabaugh, Life Coaching Client

❝ *'BE YOU' is the wake-up call we all need. If life's challenges have knocked you off course, Sidrid Rivera's powerful message will stir your soul, reset your focus, and reignite your drive. With honesty and heart, she reminds us of what truly matters—and how to reclaim it. Don't wait for another sign. This is it. Turn the page and take your next step forward.*

~ Jim Connolly, Best Selling Author of *Cooking Team Building 2.0, Rewiring How Teams Connect, Perform and Succeed*

❝ *Attending the 2024 Women's Empowerment Retreat by Sidrid Rivera Enterprises was truly life-changing—it was far more than I ever expected. The experience left me so empowered and spiritually filled that I enrolled for the 2025 retreat before I even left. Sidrid Rivera has a God-given gift for awakening purpose in women, and I'm beyond excited to be trained this year through her powerful new book, 'BE YOU'. Her words speak straight to the soul, reminding us that we are called, chosen, and enough. This journey with Sidrid continues to inspire me in both my personal and professional life."*

~ Sonia Menendez Duran, Real Estate Agent

❝ *I've had the privilege of collaborating with Sidrid Rivera through my travel agency, Jubilee Journeys, to craft unforgettable travel experiences for her. Reading her book, 'BE YOU', felt like embarking on a journey through her heart and soul. Each page radiates the same passion, authenticity, and warmth I've come to admire and know personally in our work together. Her voice shines through every story, making the book feel deeply personal and alive. I'm thrilled to partner with Sidrid Rivera Enterprises to plan their 2026 Women's Empowerment Retreat, where her inspiring message will continue to uplift and transform lives.*

~ Annabelle Valdes, Jubilee Journeys, Owner / Travel Advisor

" Desde que eras niña, siempre supe que eras diferente— tenías una luz única y una determinación que te hacía especial. No me sorprende que hayas logrado cosas que nadie más en nuestra familia, comunidad o círculo de amistades ha hecho. Siempre has sido la primera en abrir caminos, en atreverte a ser tú misma... o como dice tu libro, 'BE YOU'. Estoy tan orgullosa de la mujer valiente, empoderadora, generosa y amorosa en la que te has convertido. Me alegra saber que el mundo ahora podrá experimentar la grandeza que siempre he visto en ti. Que Dios siempre te proteja, te bendiga y te cuide en tu nuevo proyecto. Te amo mi niña.

~ Maria Correa-Maldonado, Tu Mama/Your Mom

" *I've had the privilege of knowing Sidrid Rivera for a year, and in that time, her business— Sidrid Rivera Enterprises—has transformed my life in ways I never imagined. Through her Sip with Sidrid messages, personal development classes, book clubs, coaching sessions, and powerful retreats, I have experienced deep spiritual and personal growth. Her book, 'BE YOU' has been a cornerstone in our coaching journey—filled with practical tools and empowering truths that have helped me better understand myself and step into the woman God created me to be. Attending the 2024 She Is Me Retreat and participating in her weekly Zoom sessions continues to uplift and motivate me. Sidrid's heart, wisdom, and passion for empowering women are unmatched, and I thank God every day for placing her in my life.*

~ Jennifer Wozniak Shisler, Life Coaching Client

" *I've had the blessing of knowing Sidrid Rivera through our Connect Groups at Potential Church and watching her passion shine at our SHE NIGHT women's conferences. Her heart for empowering women is undeniable, and 'BE YOU' is a beautiful reflection of that mission. Every word in her book breathes purpose, identity, and God's truth. I am truly honored to celebrate this powerful step she's taken to help women walk boldly in their full God-given potential. 'BE YOU' is more than a book—it's a divine calling lived out loud.*

~ Amber Gramling, Pastor at Potential Church

❝ *Sidrid's 'BE YOU' is a wake-up call to anyone who feels stuck living a life that doesn't feel like theirs. She challenges, inspires, and lovingly pushes you toward the version of yourself waiting to shine.*

~ Tommy Lemonade, Entrepreneur, Speaker, and Author of *When God Hands You Lemons*

❝ *'BE YOU' felt like a personal invitation to come home to myself. Sidrid's heart-centered approach reaches into the soul and reminds you that who you are is not only enough — it's divine.*

~ Debbie Saidyfye, Plant Thriving Women;
Founder, Plant Thriving Women | Nutrition & Detox Coach

❝ *Sidrid isn't just writing — she's reaching out, reminding us all that we were never meant to shrink ourselves to fit into boxes. The 'BE YOU' book is a lifeline for anyone ready to rediscover their true self.*

~ Milan Schwarzkopf, Bestseller Author, Retirement Preparation Coach, Speaker and Podcast Guest; Third Act Resources Founder

❝ BE YOU' is the kind of book that stays with you. Sidrid has poured her purpose into these pages, calling us to stop hiding and start living boldly as the masterpiece we were always created and meant to be.

~ Nicole Grey, Author of Who's the Baby? Who's the Boyfriend?

❝ This book arrived at the perfect moment. Sidrid has a way of gently but powerfully reminding you of your identity and purpose. 'BE YOU' is a must-read for anyone longing to return to their original, unfiltered self.

~ Carolyn Cahn RN, Success Coach, Author of ADHD is Your Superpower

BE YOU

Don't trade your authenticity for approval.
The world needs you to BE YOU!

Sidrid Rivera

Wisdom Eye Publishing

© 2025 by Sidrid Rivera
All Rights Reserved
ISBN: 979-8-9994848-0-2

First edition published August 2025

Published by Wisdom Eye Publishing, Chattanooga, TN

Disclaimer:

The purpose of this book is to educate and entertain. Neither the author nor publisher guarantee that anyone following the ideas, tips, suggestions, techniques, or strategies within it will become successful. The author and publisher shall have neither liability nor responsibility to anyone with respect to any loss or damage caused, or alleged to be caused, directly or indirectly, by the information contained in this book.

The author and publisher of this book is not dispensing medical advice or prescribes the use of any technique as a form of treatment for physical, emotional, all medical problems without advisor position, either directly or indirectly. The intent of this book is going to offer information of a general nature to help you in your quest for emotional, physical, and spiritual well-being. Give me a vet if you use any of the information of this book for yourself, the author and publisher has no responsibility for your actions.

Dedications

To my husband, Ricardo Rivera,

Thank you for having "Faith, Faith" in me.

Thank you for working overtime and taking on extra gigs so I wouldn't have to return to Corporate America, giving me the space to fully immerse myself in the vision God placed in my heart.

We've walked through seasons of uncertainty, sweat, fear, and tears—not knowing where this journey would lead us or whether this book would ever come to completion. And yet, through it all, your love never wavered. You stood beside me through struggles, cheered me on in my silence, and believed in me when I questioned and occasionally doubted everything.

Thank you for entrusting me with your heart and with your life... for choosing to walk this journey with me, even when the path wasn't clear. Thank you for putting yourself in a position where many men would never dare to walk, simply so I could rise.

Because of you, I am able to pursue my calling, and build a life and a business that empowers, transforms, and changes lives. Thank you for walking this journey with me, I wouldn't want anyone else by my side.

I love you infinity x's 2, always & forever.

For you. For me, & the B Boyz.

Acknowledgements

To my incredible Husband —
Ricardo, your unwavering support has been my anchor through life's highs and lows. Your love, strength, and constant belief in me gave me the courage to believe in myself, especially in the moments I thought I couldn't. Thank you for being my rock.

To my Prayer Warriors —
My Mom, my mother-in-law; Myrna, and my best friend, Graciela, your prayers carried me when my knees were too weak to bend. In my darkest hours, your faith lit a path I couldn't yet see. I am eternally grateful for your love and intercession.

Para mi bella madre —
María Correa Maldonado, eres la mujer más fuerte y resiliente que conozco. Representas lo que realmente significa ser realmente tú misma. No hay nadie como tu. Gracias por ser el ejemplo, el aliento y la definición de perseverancia y gracia. Gracias mi querida madre, por tu amor. Te amo muchísimo.

To my Sidrid Rivera Enterprises Administrative Team —
Terri Schlabaugh, Donna Frederick, Wanda Baez, Naray Cruz, & Ricardo Rivera… Thank you for being the heartbeat behind everything we do at SRE. Week

after week you show up with dedication. You serve with excellence, with grace, and most of all—with love. Please know this: I see you. I see the long nights. I feel the prayers you've pray over this vision and the way you carry the heart of this ministry as if it were your own. Because of you all, SRE continues to grow, empower, and transform lives. You are not just my team—you're my family. And I thank God for each of you. This journey would not be the same without your faith, your commitment, and your servant hearts.

To my incredible Book Coach —
Jim Connolly, Thank you for taking a chance on me. Thank you for creating space for me to be fully me. Your guidance, patience, and belief in my voice brought this dream to life, and I am forever grateful. I did it, Jim... I'm an Author!

To my extraordinary Clients —
Thank you for trusting me with your journeys and allowing me to share your stories with the world. Your courage, growth, and authenticity inspire me daily.

And most importantly, to My Lord and Savior, Jesus Christ —
This book, like my life, is yours. We wrote this together.

You whispered me in the sleepless nights, gave me peace when my spirit was restless, and reminded me I was never alone. When I doubted my purpose, you used others to confirm it. When I felt unseen, you shined your light on me. Thank you my King for choosing me to BE YOUr masterpiece!

And Finally, to YOU, the reader of this book —
I dedicate this book to you. To the woman who feels unseen, unheard, and unworthy — I see you, I was you, and sometimes I still am you. But more importantly, God sees you. You are not alone. If He could lift me from my lowest moments, He will do the same for you. I believe in you. And more than anything... you are God's masterpiece. Don't ever forget that.

Content

CHAPTER 1

   Be Real 28

CHAPTER 2

   Should We or Shouldn't We? 51

CHAPTER 3

   Pain, Purpose, Platform, Peace, or Prison . . 60

CHAPTER 4

   BE YOU 92

CHAPTER 5

   Where To Next? 104

CHAPTER 6

   Pray About It 119

CHAPTER 7

   I AM 132

CHAPTER 8

   Do Differently To Become Different 161

CHAPTER 9

   Create Your Plan 183

CHAPTER 10

Expect Differently 195

CHAPTER 11

Accept The New BEYOUtiful You 216

CHAPTER 12

Praise & Celebrate The New BEYOUtiful You . 234

INTRODUCTION

A Journey to 'BE YOU'

What if the very thing you feared the most—the thing that broke you open—was actually the key to discovering who you truly are?

That's the question at the heart of this powerful, deeply personal book. 'BE YOU' isn't just a story; it's a mirror. It reflects the struggles we often hide, the pain we bury, and the dreams we secretly doubt we are worthy of. In these pages, you'll meet a woman who dared to be real, even when it hurt—especially when it hurt. And as you journey with her, you may find the courage to uncover your own truth.

In this book, I authentically open my soul and invite you into my most vulnerable moments: the joy of unexpected pregnancy, the devastation of loss, the deep ache of betrayal, and the darkness of depression. But what makes my story unforgettable isn't just the pain—it's the way I rose from it. This book is not about pretending life is perfect. It's about choosing to live with authenticity, even when life doesn't go as planned.

Through heartbreak, infertility, and a miscarriage that nearly shattered my life, I didn't just survive—I found my purpose. I discovered that authenticity is not weakness; it is power. That forgiveness isn't forgetting—it's freedom. And that peace doesn't come from having it all together; it comes from surrendering to the One who holds it all together.

'BE YOU' will walk you through the transformation when you stop trying to be impressive and start choosing to be real. This book will remind you that the greatest breakthroughs often come after the hardest breakdowns. That rejection can be God's protection. And that the pain you've endured can either become your prison—or your platform.

This book is for every woman who has ever questioned her worth, for every person who has carried quiet grief, invisible wounds, or dreams put on hold. It's for the woman who needs to hear that her story matters, that she matters, and that she doesn't have to have it all figured out—she just has to show up as herself.

My journey from corporate America to full-time entrepreneur; from being a broken-hearted fiancée to a thriving marriage of 23 years; and from being unemployed, and in bankruptcy to becoming a successful transformational mindset coach proves that no matter what life throws at us, healing is possible, growth is inevitable, and joy is still within reach.

Whether you're struggling with your identity, navigating loss, feeling tired, hurting, hiding behind your smile, or standing at the edge of something new and terrifying… I want you to know: authenticity is worth the risk. It's in your authenticity that you will find your healing, your people, your God, and where you will discover how to truly 'BE YOU'.

This is my story, and it might BE YOUrs too.

Foreword

What if your greatest heartbreak was actually your greatest invitation? 'BE YOU' is more than a book, it's a soul-awakening. It's a mirror that dares you to stop hiding, stop striving, and start healing. In these pages, you won't find a perfectly polished life. You'll find something far more powerful: a woman who chose to rise, authentically, audaciously, and anointed.

Sidrid Rivera doesn't just tell her story; she opens a door for you to walk through your own. With raw vulnerability and radiant strength, she lets you into the sacred rooms of her life, the ones most people keep locked. And in doing so, she gives you permission to unlock yours.

You'll travel with her through loss and longing, through the ache of unanswered prayers and the whisper of divine timing. You'll see her wrestle with identity, with faith, with grief, and come out more whole, not in spite of the breaking, but because of it.

Her journey is a testimony that authenticity isn't weakness. It's where God meets us. It's where transformation begins. And it's where purpose is born.

As a relationship expert and coach, I know this truth to be universal: when a woman decides to be herself, fully and unapologetically, she doesn't just change her story, she changes the world around her.

BE YOU is not just for the woman who's hurting. It's for the woman who's healing. It's for the dreamer, the doubter, the doer, and the disciple. It's for anyone who has ever looked in the mirror and wondered, "Is this all I was made for?"

No, beloved. You were made for more. And this book will show you how to find it, not by becoming someone else, but by finally becoming yourself.

Read this book slowly. Let it speak. Let it stir. Let it shift something sacred inside you. And then go do the bravest thing you've ever done: BE YOU.

Dr. Renee Gordon-Connolly America's #1 Love & Relationship Expert International Bestselling Author & Transformational Speaker

Preface

This book is your permission to BE YOU. This book arises from the many broken places we have all experienced.

It's a testimony of pain—but also of purpose. Of trauma—but also of transformation. It's an invitation for you to remove the mask, step out of the shadows, and embrace the fullness of who you are... even the parts that still hurt. Because your story—even the messy, raw, and heartbreaking parts—they're powerful and they matter. Your story can guide others to healing, just like mine did.

As you turn the pages of this book, I encourage you to be open—to feel, reflect, and perhaps even release the things you've been carrying for far too long. Let this book remind you that you are not alone, that you are seen, that you are loved, and, most importantly, that you are already enough—just as you are.

This book isn't about perfection. It's not about having all the answers or pretending everything is fine... because it's not. It's about showing up as the real, raw, and redeemed version of yourself—even when life has broken you in two. This is a journey of rediscovery, of releasing shame, of embracing grace, and of finding strength in vulnerability and courage in truth.

This book encourages you to delve deeper. It discusses the powerful, life-altering decision to forgive. "To forgive is to set a prisoner free and discover that the prisoner was you." This book teaches you how to transform your pain. Pain can become your purpose, your peace, your platform… or your prison. The choice is yours. This book guides you towards prayer—because when your hands are tied and you feel trapped in a season with no way out, prayer is your lifeline.

This book will ask you, "Who are you?" And not just who the world says you are, but who God says you are. Understanding who you are is the foundation of becoming who you're meant to be. Too often, we let the noise of others shape our identity—and we lose ourselves. That's why so many people feel lost. They've strayed from the path God designed uniquely for them. But this book reminds you how to come back home—to your heart, to your truth, to your purpose, to your God.

This book will walk with you step by step, helping you create a plan. It will teach you how to set goals that align with God and your heart's desires, so you can begin to expect differently, live differently, and receive differently. It encourages you to boldly accept the new BEYOUtiful you, because the moment you accept yourself, you become BEYOUtiful.

So, if you've ever been brokenhearted, faced depression, lost someone you loved, felt unseen, unheard, or misunderstood, questioned your worth, or silently struggled to find your place, then this book is for you.

And last but certainly not least, this book gives you permission to praise and celebrate the new BeYoutiful you. Because as you grow, evolve, and transform, you deserve to celebrate. You deserve to rejoice in the woman you've become. The more you praise and celebrate your life, the more there is in life to celebrate.

Know this: you're holding more than a book. You're holding my heart, my healing, my testimony, my truth. And through it all, my hope is that you'll find your own truth… and the freedom to fully, unapologetically, and fearlessly BE YOU.

So, welcome. You're exactly where you need to be. Let's take this journey together. Let's rediscover what it truly means to BE YOU! Welcome to your transformation. Welcome to your healing. Welcome to your breakthrough. Welcome to becoming the most real, free, and BeYoutiful version of YOU. I can't wait to celebrate YOU!

CHAPTER 1

Be Real

"Forget about being impressive and commit to being real because being real is impressive."

~ Jonathan Harnisch ~

When I first came across this quote, "Forget about being impressive and commit to being real because being real is impressive" it spoke to the deepest part of my soul. The truth is, being real isn't always easy—but it's always worth it. To me, being real means standing in your truth, being transparent, and showing up as the person God uniquely designed you to be. It's not about perfection. It's not about performance. It's about presence—living fully and honestly in the moment, even when that moment feels uncertain or vulnerable. Being real means you don't have to hide. You don't have to shrink yourself or fit into anyone else's mold. You get to show up, flaws and all, and say: "This is me." But let me ask you... **"What does being real mean to you?"**

For me, the journey of being real began with one of the most intimate and pivotal conversations of my life. It was the year 2000 when I met my husband, Ricky. From the moment we met, there was a connection I couldn't deny.

In February 2000, I met my husband, Ricky, at a nightclub, and after two years of dating, we decided we wanted to get married, so in March 2002, we tied the knot. But before we got married, I had to tell him the truth: that I may never be able to have children. Due to reproductive issues, motherhood wasn't a promise in my future—and if that was something his heart longed for, I didn't want to stand in the way. It was a moment of honesty that could have changed everything. But I chose to be real with him because love deserves the truth, and I promised to always show up as my full, authentic self.

At the time, I wasn't even sure I wanted to be a mother. I told everyone, including myself, that motherhood wasn't something I desired. But God… had a different plan.

Well, after a few years of marriage, guess who got pregnant? OMG… I couldn't believe it because, as I mentioned earlier, we had reproductive issues trying to conceive. No matter how much we tried or what we did, those pregnancy tests kept coming back negative.

Until one day, when we least expected it, there it was... a positive result. I was pregnant, and I didn't even know it.

I used to work for a gynecologist and a maternal-fetal medicine (MFM) group, and one day when I arrived at work, one of the MFM physicians looked at me and said, with a happy face, "Congratulations." Let me help you visualize this conversation...

Sidrid: What are you congratulating me for? Did I get a raise? (laughing & excited)

Dr. A: No, I'm congratulating you because you're pregnant. Aren't you?

Sidrid: What?? Aaaahhh No, that's not what I'm aware of (with a clueless look).

Dr. A: Are you sure?

Sidrid: Ahhh yeah, last time I checked, still nothing.

Dr. A: When was the last time you checked? (Just in case you were wondering, everyone in my office knew Ricky and I were trying to get pregnant. We are a tight work family.)

Sidrid: Ummm, about a week ago?

Dr A: He turned to his medical assistant and said, "Can you please go get her a pregnancy test?"

Sidrid: Wait... what? What's happening right now?

Dr. A: Girl, you are glowing from head to toe. The minute you walked into the office, I noticed a shine all over you. I've been in this business for a long time, and I can tell when I see a pregnant woman, and you, my dear, are definitely pregnant without knowing it. So, I'm going to prove it to you. Please take this pregnancy test and come back to us with the results. I'll be waiting for you in the ultrasound room to see how baby Rivera is doing.

Right then and there, I found out that I was pregnant. I couldn't believe it; I couldn't believe he was right. My heart sank—I was pregnant. Oh, enchiladas (one of my crazy sayings), I was pregnant! After several years of trying, WE DID IT! Tears streamed down my face. I didn't even know what to do with myself. I was shaking; I was excited, nervous, shocked, and over the moon. I couldn't stop saying, "I am pregnant! Oh enchiladas, I am pregnant!" Then, it dawned on me that I had to tell my husband we were pregnant. I didn't even know how to tell him. The office staff were all screaming and jumping up and down with excitement for both of us. I went into that ultrasound room, and there was Dr. A with a tear on his face, waiting and ready to show me baby Rivera.

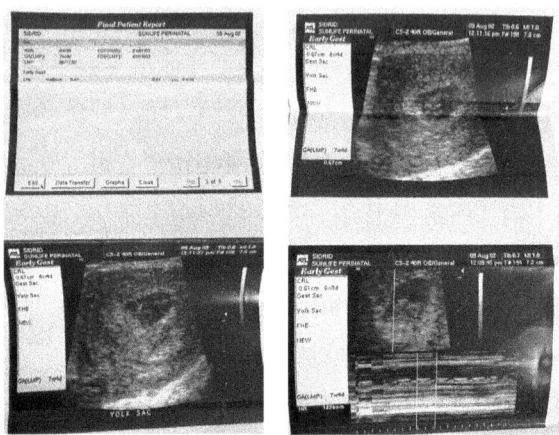

These are the cutest ultrasound images I had of baby Rivera, and I couldn't wait to show them to Ricky.

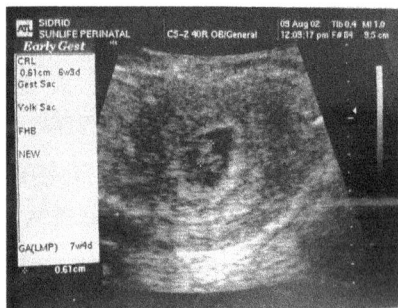

I was sent home early from work to think and prepare how I was going to tell Ricky. But before I left the parking lot, I sat in my car and cried for a good ten minutes. I was in awe and so grateful to God that we had done it—we were going to be parents.

I wiped away my tears and drove to Ross, a department store in Florida. I bought the cutest little outfit with matching booties and found a onesie that said, "I love you, Daddy." I placed everything in a decorative baby bag and waited for my husband to leave work. I was so excited that my hands were shaking. When Ricky got home, I sat him down and told him our lives were about to change. He thought we had won the lottery (and in a sense, we did). I handed him the bag, and I'll never forget the look in his eyes when he saw the pregnancy test and the images of baby Rivera. He pulled me closer and held me tight for a few minutes. We didn't say a word; I knew what he felt then. It took him a minute, but once he was ready, he looked through the bag and saw the onesies, the booties, and the cute outfit. At that moment, for the second time in my life, I saw a tear fall down his face. They were tears of joy, gratitude, and love for this small creation living inside me. We were both extremely emotional and very present with each other. Those were tears we never thought we would experience. We were so excited and incredibly grateful that baby Rivera would join our family soon, until it didn't.

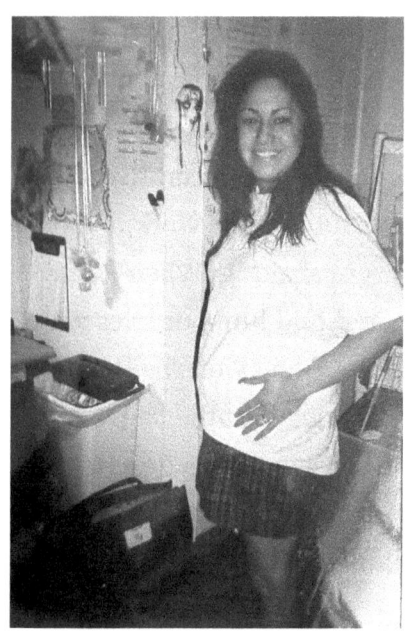

Unfortunately, the worst had happened. At five months, during our OBGYN appointment, a sonogram confirmed that baby Rivera's heartbeat had stopped. I experienced an internal miscarriage, which meant our baby had died inside my uterus, and the only way to remove the baby was for the doctor to perform a dilation and curettage (also known as a D&C). For those of you reading this book who are not aware of what a dilation and curettage involves, it's a medical procedure used to scrape and remove the baby's tissue from the inner lining of the uterus.

I don't know if you have ever experienced a miscarriage after desperately trying to become a mom. Still, if you have, you'll understand the excruciating pain that fills your heart afterward. Your body becomes numb, and you truly think you will never feel again. Every part of me shut down, including my mind. Trying to climb out of what felt like the pit of hell seemed impossible.

What I didn't realize back then was that being real doesn't just mean celebrating the good parts of your story. It means being honest about the painful parts, too. The broken places. The chapters you never thought you'd have to write. There's something about pain—deep, soul-wrenching pain—that strips away all the layers we've carefully built to protect ourselves. And in the aftermath of my miscarriage, that's precisely what happened to me. My smile faded. My voice fell silent. And for the first time in a long time, I didn't want to be seen… not how people were used to seeing me.

If you've never had a miscarriage, thank God and pray you never do. The only thing I believe that compares to a miscarriage is losing a child because that's precisely what happens. Getting pregnant wasn't easy for us; we had to go through numerous cycles and doses of Clomid for fertility treatments, and we underwent IVF, along with countless doctor appointments, ovulation tracking, and temperature check-ups, to name a few. So, after experiencing a miscarriage at five months, after everything we went through to get pregnant, let me say that trying to express the pain, frustration, and devastation was extremely difficult; the pain was unbearable. I didn't think there were words to explain what I was feeling or what I was experiencing physically, emotionally, and mentally. Depression took over, and I couldn't escape it.

I experienced deep depression for a long time. I felt angry, empty, in disbelief, guilty, lonely, sad, unworthy, and I isolated myself. I viewed myself as a failure. My emotions were chaotic, and I had no idea how to cope with the emotional turmoil I was facing. Hormonal shifts intensified my feelings; some days I could get out of bed and eat something, while most days I curled up in a ball in the corner of my bedroom or huddled in the shower. Several women would visit me, wanting to "help" by comforting me, but nothing seemed effective. They tried to "encourage me" by sharing their experiences with similar situations or assuring me that "everything will be okay and things will improve." One person even said, "miscarriages are normal; many women go through one or two of them, and then suddenly, they get pregnant. You'll conceive again."

All the encouragement only made me angrier. I felt like I needed everyone to leave me alone. Deep down,

I could hear myself yelling, screaming, "LEAVE ME ALONE, JUST SHUT UP." Yes, I said it. That's how I felt, and that's what I wanted to shout out at times. I was broken, and my true self wanted everyone to SHUT UP. But I didn't; I didn't tell anyone to shut up or to leave me alone. I didn't tell them that they weren't helping me; I didn't tell anyone anything. I shut down, cried, and hated the world and everything in it. I didn't have enough energy to say anything; I barely spoke. I know, right? Me not talking? There's something wrong if I'm not speaking.

Have you ever felt that way? Have you ever wanted to tell someone what they said didn't matter? Didn't their words make you feel any better? Have you ever wanted to tell someone to be quiet because no matter how often they said they understood you, they didn't? Have you ever wanted to ask someone to leave you alone because just hearing their voice made you want to curl into a ball and cry for days? Well, that's how I felt, and finally one day that's exactly what I said. I just couldn't hold it any longer.

Emotionally, I didn't want to hear that they, too, had experienced a miscarriage or that miscarriage was "normal for women." It felt as if they were trying to minimize or dismiss my feelings, my emotions, and my painful experience. I needed to confront this horrible pain and the emptiness within me. Now, don't get me wrong; I knew they were trying to help, and I understood they meant no harm, but they weren't helping. Their encouragement made me feel worse because I couldn't bounce back like everyone expected me to. All I wanted to say was, "Please stop, please go away, and please leave me alone." But God knew that what I wanted wasn't what I needed.

Needless to say, after many "encouraging" words and stories, I did it. I yelled out so loudly… "STOP! Please STOP telling me about your miscarriages; STOP telling me how this is normal and that many women go through it. STOP telling me that I will be okay, and please STOP telling me we can try again. Just STOP!" My sudden yelling wasn't something anyone expected. Still, I thank God everyone understood that I was experiencing a devastating loss, and they realized I was just not myself… or was I? Was this the beginning of me understanding what true authenticity means? What is being honest with those around you truly about? Was this experience the start of discovering what I was no longer willing to hide… ME, my thoughts, my desires, my dreams, my emotions, my feelings, and my beliefs. What if this was the beginning of discovering the real me?

When I finally let that truth out, when I released all the pressure I had been carrying, something surprising happened—people listened. Not to their voices, but to mine. And not just the words I spoke, but the ones I couldn't talk. The ones I had buried beneath my silence and my tears.

That moment of honesty, that release, became a powerful turning point in my life because that is when I realized what authenticity is.

It's not just about being bold and confident when life is good—it's about being honest when it's not. It's about saying, "I'm not okay" and not apologizing for it. It's about giving yourself permission to feel, to grieve, to question… and to heal in your own time.

It's also about recognizing that God's presence isn't absent in our suffering. Sometimes, He's quiet. Sometimes, He's still. But He's always there. And even though I wasn't ready to reach out to Him right away, I knew—deep down—that He had not left me. He was just sitting with me in the silence, waiting for me to be ready.

In that season of stillness and pain, I discovered something sacred: sometimes, the most authentic thing you can do is to fall apart—so that you can begin again.

I believe this was probably the first time these women got to see my true self. I shared with them that my emotional distress made it infuriating to listen. I didn't want to hear that miscarriages were normal or that they or a friend of theirs had experienced one. I didn't want to listen to those stories, and I surely didn't want to discuss my own experiences. We sat down together, and I was genuine and honest with them. I simply told them, "If you want to come visit me, just sit with me in silence, or eat with me in silence, or watch a movie with me quietly, and please definitely pray for me. Pray for me a lot because I was broken, I was hurting, and I was afraid—afraid that I wouldn't be able to pull myself out of this one.

I apologized to the ladies if I came across as rude or mean when I yelled. I was expressing the rawness of my aching heart. We all knew that once I decided to surrender my pain, my heart, my depression, my loneliness, and my sadness to God, I would eventually "ultimately" rise above my emotional turmoil. "Ultimately," being the key word, this pain requires healing time. We all understood that to be true, but we also knew it would take a while. Deep down, I acknowledged that God could help me; I didn't have the strength to reach Him. Or maybe I was genuinely angry with God for what had occurred, which held me back from engaging with Him. Perhaps it was a mixture of all my emotions and thoughts, making me a hot mess.

Sometimes, your authenticity requires solitude, while at other times, it envelops you in genuine love and peace. To experience both, you must be true to yourself and those around you, even when challenging. I needed some time alone, yet I also longed for love from my family and friends during this harrowing period in our lives. It was when I shouted, "STOP!" that my family and friends recognized my authenticity. At that moment, they realized they weren't truly helping; they weren't hearing my silence or listening beyond their voices. It was then that they asked, "How can I help?" and told me they were around if I needed anything.

It took about a year... a full year of pain, silence, reflection, and rebuilding to start breathing again— truly breathing. Depression tried to convince me that I would never smile again, that the sun would never rise for me. But slowly and gently, God reminded me that healing was still possible. It happened in the quiet moments. During those quiet nights that I felt most grateful for having my husband by my side, hearing him pray over his wife helped reminded me he had not given up on me or us. In his consistent, loving voice checking in on me during lunch breaks. In the prayers whispered by faithful women who never gave up on me, even when I had given up on myself. In the subtle nudge of gratitude that found its way into my broken heart. Gratitude became the key that unlocked the chains of depression, one moment at a time. It was in those moments that I realize there was a whole world out there I could still choose to engage in. Every day, I choose to be thankful for something different. I began being grateful for my husband, and my family, and my prayer warriors, for the food I starting eating, the water running down my back when I showered, the hug from a friend, the call from a loved one, for stepping outside my room, for Hallmark movies I would watch, for taking walks with my husband, and the cream he would bring me. It was GRATITUDE that helped me release the demon of depression.

During those quiet, lonely moments, I had time to think, and it was then that I realized that life is a choice. I had to decide whether I would be grateful for my life and the future I could still create, or whether I would remain stuck in my emotional funk. Was I going to surrender my emotional struggles to God and choose to move forward, or was I going to carry my depression with me every single day and live in misery? I chose to let go and let God care for my broken heart. I decided to appreciate what I had, rather than focusing too much on what I didn't have (yet). I chose to be thankful for the man God blessed me with and to share my life with him. I was determined to free myself from the depression that could have dragged me down mentally, emotionally, spiritually, and eventually physically into despair.

I chose to draw closer to God, as he was my only hope. I chose to let go of my anger. I believe everything happens for a reason, even if we don't like or understand it. I trusted that my God had a better plan for Ricky and me. I chose to heal; as challenging as it was, I chose to heal. I chose to matter, even though I wasn't a mom. I chose not to allow my lack of motherhood to define the woman I was meant to become. And I chose to believe that not being a mother didn't mean I wasn't deserving of greatness. I released those negative emotions and filled my life with moments that brought me laughter, made my heart happy, brought me joy, empowered me, and excited me. I chose to live for myself, for the man I love, and for the God I serve. I chose to live for my family and the families who consistently prayed for me, for us. I chose to live for all the women who have experienced or will experience miscarriages, as this misfortune symbolically connects us. I chose to live so I can share this story with you so that you know you are not alone in this world of infertility, loneliness, sadness, darkness, depression, anger, and fear. I see you because I am you. I see you because I have been you. I chose to live so that when you face your difficult times, no matter what they are, you know that I am here for you and that I truly see you because I've been there too. But do you know what's even greater than me seeing you? That God sees you! He sees you just as He saw me. He sees all of us!

This experience has taught me how to be real with myself and with others. We all need to be genuine with each other, respectful of one another, of course, but authentically honest as well. It should matter to us to be truthful and real with each other. Don't we want people to see the real us so that there is no confusion in this world? We shouldn't allow others to have a false image of us. I want people to see me for who I truly am: to understand my beliefs, what I stand for, what my values are, and who I believe in. We all want to be recognized; it's in our nature, deep within our being, and embedded in our souls. When we aren't genuinely real with people, they tend to create an image of us that often doesn't reflect who we really are.

We live in a world where people wear masks—not just to protect themselves, but to be accepted, to be liked, to avoid judgment. But here's the truth: masks might protect you, but they also prevent you from being seen. They keep you disconnected, not just from others, but from your own heart.

We can't connect with certain individuals because we are usually trying to please people we don't even like in the first place. When you are authentically true to yourself, you'll find the right people to connect with because they will also be genuine. It's like trying to fit a puzzle piece into the wrong spot; it will never work. No matter how much we try, if we try to fit in with a group that isn't similar to who we are, it won't happen. One of us will eventually change, and if you look at yourself and realize that you don't like what you see, it could be because you've altered your authenticity to please others.

The lack of authenticity allows individuals to form their own image of who you are, and if they don't like what they see, they won't connect with you. When you are genuinely real, there aren't multiple versions of you for different people to perceive. Everyone sees you for who you truly are, enabling you to connect with the right people—those who are just like you, who enjoy being around you, and who are also authentic. You see, authenticity attracts authenticity. You can't fake authenticity; you can't pretend to be authentic—people see right through it. Those who are not authentic recognize it, too. Authenticity occurs when different individuals all perceive the same version of who you are. They all have the same experiences when you are present; you make them feel the same way, and they all love and appreciate you for your uniqueness.

One early afternoon, I was chatting with my husband about life—probably some silly nonsense that didn't really matter—when his cell phone rang. As soon as he began to talk, I glanced at him and said (let's call him Bobby), "Tell Bobby I said hello." Ricky smiled and asked, "How do you know it was Bobby?" As I walked away, I replied, "I just do." I recognized who it was because of the tone of Ricky's voice, his gestures, his vocabulary, and his manner of speaking automatically shifted. I could tell he was talking to a man, and in seconds, I knew it was Bobby. It was as if he transformed into a different person. It was the funniest thing. When Ricky finished, I asked him, "Why do you speak differently when you're talking to one of your guy friends?" His response was very genuine. He simply said, "I don't know; it's a guy thing." It took me a minute, but then I realized I had seen many other guys do the same. When they gather or chat on the phone, their pitch changes, the words they use change and even their body language shifts. Their voices get deeper, they laugh at the silliest jokes, and you hear words coming out of their mouths that you don't often hear. Occasionally, they give each other hugs that seem like they're about to break each other's backs. It's pretty funny to watch. But it's their authenticity—it's men being men, expressing their masculinity. The next time you're out with a few male friends, pay attention to how they greet each other, how high they lift their arms for hugs, handshakes, or high-fives. Listen to how they speak and interact; you might chuckle because you'll realize that what I'm saying is true: its men being their authentic selves around other men!

Authenticity comes at a cost; it presents both advantages and disadvantages to being genuinely authentic around others. Some people may not like you, appreciate you, or connect with you, and honestly, that's their personal issue, not yours. I've spent considerable time improving myself and not letting others affect me anymore. I am now completely fine with those who choose not to like me because of my authenticity. This simply confirms that some individuals prefer inauthentic, fake, and insincere characters in their lives because they share those same traits. Personally, I don't do fake, and I lack the time or energy to engage with inauthentic people. None of us do, so don't settle for those types of "friends, family members, spouses, children, bosses, etc."

Authenticity involves aligning your values, ideas, dreams, desires, and actions with your true self. It's important for us to be individuals with principles and beliefs, and to share those values, ideas, and beliefs with others. Our relationships, being honest to each other, and our integrity should matter to us, even if others disagree. If someone doesn't like you or doesn't want to BE YOUr friend because you are genuinely real and honest, you should find peace in that. There will always be people who do not appreciate your honesty; it's essential to accept this as part of their own authenticity. God desires us to be truthful with one another. Therefore, when we meet individuals who do not share our values and beliefs and do not appreciate our authenticity, recognizing that as their own truth can help us move forward, lying is an abomination to the Lord, so stay true to yourself. You don't have to change who you are because someone holds different beliefs. God grants each of us the free will to decide who we want to be, whom we wish to serve, whom we choose to love, and what we want to believe in. Authenticity is about being honest with yourself and others while respecting everyone else's authenticity as well.

There will be moments of disagreement and times when we're out of sync with one another. However, we must still respect each other, love one another, and appreciate our unique qualities. If my authenticity makes you uncomfortable, consider reflecting on why that is. Could it be that you're not being true to yourself, or perhaps that my values, ideas, and beliefs differ from yours? And that's perfectly okay. Often, when people feel uneasy about my authenticity, it's because they aren't being authentic with others, or even worse, they aren't being real with themselves.

However, there are times when people feel uncomfortable with my authenticity because they don't share my beliefs, value the things I value, or sometimes dislike my ideas. Occasionally, they don't believe in the one God that I do. I've learned that it's okay when people disagree; that's part of growing up, gaining wisdom, and choosing love, kindness, and understanding. We shouldn't expect others to believe, value, like, or desire what we do. How boring would it be if we were all the same? Believing the same things, wanting the same outcomes, liking the same stuff? That is not how we were created, we were purposely created to be different, to be our own unique, authentic selves, a divine masterpiece. What if we were more Christ-like, and not so much more like one another? We need to respect each other's differences, and if for any reason you can't seem to appreciate someone's uniqueness, well, this world is big enough that we can find someone else to connect with. As long as we're being true to ourselves and those around us, respect becomes second nature. Respect is about having a deep admiration for someone or something that brings out their abilities, qualities, or achievements. It's about treating others how you would like to be treated. Does that sound familiar?

CHAPTER 2

Should We, or Shouldn't We?

"To forgive is to set a prisoner free and discover that the prisoner was you.."

~ Lewis B Smedes ~

About 12 years ago, me and one of my closest friends, whom I've known for over 20 years, were discussing about forgiveness. Unfortunately, she found out that her husband had been having an affair for about five years. As she shared her story, she often said she would never forgive him. Each time she said what he had done, she declared, "I will never forgive him." I understood she was speaking from a deep, painful, dark place, so I let her vent and express all the emotions she was feeling. She needed that. I could hear the pain, anger, and suffering in her voice. I could empathize with her feelings.

So when she asked me, "You wouldn't be able to forgive him either, right?" she was extremely surprised and a bit upset when I replied, "No, eventually I would forgive him." She looked at me as if I were crazy. You see, I could relate to her situation; I had gone through a very similar painful breakup. She said, "Wait, what? You would forgive him?" I responded, "Yes, eventually I would forgive him. In fact, I have forgiven him." She became upset because she thought I was taking her husband's side, but I told her, "I'm not taking his side, and I'm not taking your side. I'm speaking from my experience. I'm actually taking God's side."

In August 1998, after seven years of dating my ex and just a month before our wedding, I caught my ex-fiancée in bed with another woman. Everything was paid for; people were flying in from all over the country, and I thought we were all set. One late evening, I arrived at his apartment to surprise him, but to my surprise, there was a woman in his bed whom he had been dating for about a year. I was devastated, destroyed, angry, and sad, to say the least. I couldn't believe what was happening. After seven years of loving and dating this person, getting to know him and spending time with his family and friends, I was stunned by his deceitful behavior.

I felt abandoned, angry, and embarrassed. Embarrassed because people were coming to our wedding to celebrate our "happiness". Why didn't I see this coming? Why did he do this? How could I have missed it? These are just a few questions that constantly run through my mind. I felt as if I had been blinded, struck in the head and heart with a baseball bat over and over again. I was so heartbroken that I didn't sleep or eat for days—actually, for months. There were times when my chest felt so heavy and tight that I couldn't breathe. I struggled to fall asleep and could barely catch my breath. I experienced such a mix of emotions. Everything we worked so hard for was over. I knew that the dreams, the plans, and the future we had envisioned together were all gone. In the blink of an eye, everything was destroyed. The life I thought we would live had changed instantly, and I had no idea what was next. I was about to have a different life; change was unavoidable.

Why? Because there was no way that I was going to forgive him.

I found the courage to say goodbye, and I left him, but forgiveness took time. I knew I needed to start over. So, I did. In October 1998, I moved from Brooklyn, NY, to Hollywood, FL. With $40 in my pocket and the clothes on my back, I moved in with a distant cousin. My cousin, Sunny welcomed me with open arms and helped me restart my life. He assisted me in finding a new job, making new friends, and buying my first car, and he often cooked for me. He loved preparing delicious Puerto Rican meals for the both of us. We became each other's companions, and Sunny helped me rediscover myself. He reminded me every day that even though my heart was broken and I often felt lost, he believed I would get through this stronger than ever, and eventually, I did.

I had moments when I was upset, and there were many days and nights when I would reflect on those memories, struggling to forgive. But would I ever truly forgive him? Would I harbor hatred for him forever because of what he did? Of course not. This was another challenge I faced, helping me realize how crucial authenticity is in our lives. I used to view hardships as obstacles to overcome quickly. However, experiencing the pain of a broken heart forced me to slow down and examine who I was. I needed to confront aspects of myself that I had previously avoided, and in that raw honesty, I discovered how liberating it is to show up as myself fully. Enduring that heartache taught me that authenticity isn't just a choice; it's essential. It's the foundation of genuine relationships and true fulfillment. Now, I embrace it wholeheartedly because I know that being authentic is the only way to live and connect with others truly.

After I was no longer in denial or shock, angry or depressed, once I stopped isolating myself out of embarrassment for what had happened, and as I realized I wanted true fulfillment, I <u>chose</u> to heal.

Eventually, my heart began to mend, and I started to love myself again—not because of what anyone else had done or said, but because I finally felt worthy of it. That blend of forgiveness and self-love was like stepping out of a storm and into the sunlight, feeling free and whole. It was as if I had finally lost a weight I had carried for far too long. There was this incredible release, like my heart had been holding its breath, and I could finally exhale. I had reclaimed my peace. It was then that I became the real me! It was then that I understood that authenticity was essential for me to become the woman I was meant to be.

We have to reach a point of acceptance, realizing that no one should hold so much power over us that we lose ourselves, our peace, or the people we are destined to become. Forgiveness isn't about excusing the pain—it's about safeguarding our well-being, our sanity, and the life we were meant to live. Yes, the pain can be intense, and anger is real when we're betrayed. However, our inner peace, our life's purpose, and our connection to something greater isn't worth sacrificing. By forgiving, we free ourselves to move forward, whole and resilient.

When we choose to forgive, we move forward, find closure, and free ourselves from the emotions that pull us away from the future we are meant to fulfill. Forgiveness is a powerful choice, not to excuse the actions of those who have hurt us, but to reclaim control over our mental and emotional well-being. It's about refusing to let the heartbreaker, the abuser, or the aggressor continue to hold power over us. By forgiving, we release their grip on us, allowing ourselves the space to focus on our growth, healing, and happiness.

Holding onto anger or resentment keeps us tied to those who have wronged us, giving them ongoing influence over our lives. However, forgiveness severs that tie. It doesn't mean we condone, forget, or invite more harm—it simply means we choose not to let someone else's actions dictate our peace or our life's journey. In forgiving, we grant ourselves the ultimate gift of freedom, breaking free from another's wrongdoing and reclaiming our power to live fully.

If you're wondering how I ended the conversation with my friend, I simply said, 'In the end, forgiveness is a choice, and I chose to forgive. I wasn't going to let anger define my future or dwell on painful emotions by questioning why it happened, what I could have done differently, or what I did wrong. I decided there must be truth in what the Bible says about forgiveness, finding joy, and trusting that God has something better for us. I'm so thankful every day that I chose to forgive, embrace joy, and live fully—because God did have something much better for me, my husband Ricardo.

And if I may be real with you—and maybe even brag a little—my ex eventually noticed the new me I was becoming. He saw that my life was now truly "all about me." I was taking better care of myself, both physically and mentally. I transformed my physique by eating healthier, toning up, and losing weight; I became financially independent, moved into a cozy apartment, adopted a puppy, and found new strength mentally and spiritually. I felt and looked incredible. After all the work I had done to rebuild myself, he tried to come back. When I say he tried, I mean he truly made an effort. For almost two years, he sent flowers to my job and home, showed up at my workplace, even applied for a job where I worked, and eventually got hired, making his way into management, where I had to work with him daily. Ohhhh enchiladas! But eventually his actual intentions and his true colors were revealed, and he was fired.

I understood my friend's pain deeply and could relate to what she was experiencing. However, I also knew that if she wanted to find peace—and be open to Jesus' forgiveness—she would eventually need to forgive him. In the eyes of God, or whatever higher power you believe in, we are all imperfect and have made mistakes. None of us are free from flaws. So, why not release the burden and let God handle those who have wronged us? Consider this: how can we ask God and others for forgiveness when we choose to withhold it ourselves?

I reminded her that forgiveness isn't easy and doesn't happen overnight. It takes time and support from God and others. However, the sooner we let go, the sooner we can heal and become who we're meant to be. If you want to draw closer to God, forgiveness is a step along that path—it's a way to receive mercy and grace. It's through the pain you can find your purpose, and it's within your purpose that you can release the pain.

Let me show you what I mean...

CHAPTER 3

Pain, Purpose, Platform, Peace, or Prison

"Transform your pain into your purpose, your platform, your peace, or your prison, the choice is yours!"

~ Sidrid Rivera ~

During one of my coaching sessions, a client—let's call her Debbie—shared that she constantly went above and beyond to help others, driven by her desire to be liked by everyone. Even when she didn't particularly enjoy someone's company or didn't want to fulfill a request, she would still say 'yes' simply to avoid any negative opinions. Debbie rarely said 'no' because she feared she would be perceived negatively. When she didn't have the time or had other plans, she would try to reschedule her own commitments. Often, she even canceled her plans to accommodate someone else's needs. Debbie needed approval from others and wanted them to view her as capable of assisting anyone. Do you know anyone like this? Could this possibly BE YOU?

While God calls us to help others, Debbie's motivation wasn't truly about service; it was rooted in her own insecurities. When insecurity takes root, authenticity cannot flourish. Insecurity can be toxic, blocking the genuine connections and peace that arise when we help others from a place of confidence and compassion.

It's evident that Debbie's desire for everyone to like her was unrealistic and setting goals like this can hinder us from living authentically. Authenticity involves being genuine with us and others, which begins with establishing realistic goals that reflect our abilities, skills, health, and the time frame we allocate for ourselves. Realistic goals enable us to outline the necessary steps to achieve them, fostering growth without leading us toward failure. Goals should be measurable so we can monitor our progress. Without these quantifiable steps, we risk undermining our own success, resulting in feelings of defeat and unworthiness. As Benjamin Franklin wisely stated, "If you fail to plan, you plan to fail." Realistic goals focus on developing a clear, step-by-step plan. For instance, aiming for everyone to like you is unrealistic because 'like' is an emotion that fluctuates with circumstances. Depending on unrealistic goals to satisfy our sense of worth often leaves us feeling empty and unfulfilled. Conversely, establishing realistic, attainable goals rooted in self-awareness cultivates confidence and a sense of purpose.

Many people struggle with confidence, self-love, and self-worth, often seeking validation from those who don't genuinely care for them. This need for external approval causes many to compromise their authenticity, prioritizing the opinions of others over their own desires and well-being. We become so focused on pleasing others, yearning to be liked—or even loved—that we neglect our own dreams, happiness, relationships, and spiritual growth. Living to fulfill others' expectations isn't truly living; it's allowing others to shape our lives, ultimately leaving us unfulfilled and distant from the love and peace we deeply crave.

True authenticity is about discovering inner peace. It means no longer needing to please everyone or seek constant approval. With that inner peace, you're no longer consumed by what others think, how they perceive you, or whether they approve. That anxiety diminishes, replaced by a calm that surpasses all understanding—a peace that enables you to embrace who you truly are without hesitation or fear.

Consider the following: Do I have inner peace? Do I feel affected if someone doesn't like me? Do others' opinions cause me anxiety, sadness, or even depression? How do I react when someone dislikes being my friend or speaks negatively about me? Reflect on whether you find peace in the knowledge that what they say isn't true and isn't worth your time or energy, or do you need to "fix" others' views? Are you disappointed or upset when you're not invited to social events?

Please understand me; these situations can be hurtful, sad, and overwhelming, and it's natural to feel affected. However, when we know why people act as they do—especially when their actions challenge our hearts, minds, or spirits—we find that they no longer hold power over us. You become more focused on their behavior, realizing that your peace is far more valuable and essential to your well-being. By prioritizing this peace, you create a buffer that shields your heart and soul from the harm others may intend, anchoring yourself to what truly matters.

Peace arrives in various forms, and we can invite it into our lives in ways that resonate most with us. For some, peace may come from mindfulness meditation, quiet moments of self-reflection, yoga, spirituality, or a connection with God. The word "peace" comes from the Latin term "tranquility," which fundamentally refers to calmness. Whether through meditation, solitude, yoga, spirituality, or connecting with God through prayer or scripture, each practice leads us toward the calmness and deep peace we all seek.

If you search for "Where does peace come from?", you'll often encounter answers that point to a higher power. Google states: "Peace is a product of God's design, much like creation itself." Both spiritual texts and modern wisdom suggest that peace has a divine origin. Therefore, whether you discover your peace through yoga, the universe, meditation, a motivational podcast, a higher power, an inspiring book, or God himself, these moments of tranquility are essential. Taking the time to cultivate this inner peace is vital for leading a balanced fulfilling life.

For me, peace comes from meditating on God's word and being in His presence. Spending quiet moments listening to God and reflecting on His word brings me a profound sense of peace and happiness. When I am grounded in this peaceful spirit, I feel love, joy, security, comfort, worthiness, and confidence. I'm ready for the day and prepared for whatever comes my way, with a clear mind and vivid thoughts. My goals, values, and beliefs are clear, and I focus on what I need to accomplish, making decisions confidently rather than being in doubt. My vision is sharp, and my heart, mind, and spirit align with that vision.

The assurance that God will provide, guide, love, protect, forgive, and be present for me fills my life with peace and joy. Despite hardships like marital struggles, financial challenges, family issues, job setbacks, health battles, and other trials, finding peace in God transforms life into a better place. Life's problems, although real, feel less overwhelming as His peace grounds me. This inner calm renders others' opinions and judgments insignificant, liberating me from their definitions of who I am. Living in God's authentic peace shifts my focus to what He is doing in my life instead of seeking validation from others. In this space, I discover true, genuine friendships drawn nearby God's hand. With Him, I am often "in the right place at the right time" and open to His blessings and guidance.

Peace lays the groundwork for discovering your path, purpose, passion, and goals. When you embrace God's true peace, you can focus on yourself and the authentic desires of your heart. Free from the need to please others, your mind expands to pursue the things you love, the dreams you hold dear, and the activities that bring you joy. With a peaceful heart, you gain clarity about whether you are truly living the life you have always desired, the life you have always envisioned, or the life others have chosen for you to live.

For many of us, life can feel as if it is simply "happening" to us. However, looking deeper, we can realize that life is happening for us, not to us. What does this mean? Although challenges arise, we hold the power to make choices that can transform our lives. We can decide what we want to change: the new directions to pursue, the jobs we aspire to have, the partner we want to marry, the schools we want to attend, the careers we dream of, the values we choose to uphold, the people we love, and the places we want to travel to—just to name a few. If you're not fully satisfied with where you are now, remember—you, and only you, can create the change you seek.

Have you ever asked yourself, "Am I truly where I'm meant to be? Am I living the life I've always dreamt of? Am I in alignment with the true desires of my heart, or even better, with God's purpose for my life?" These are profound questions—ones that many of us rarely consider. Perhaps we avoid them because we're not ready for the answers. Deep down, we might sense that we're not living the life we truly want, not aligned with our heart's desires, and may not even recognize our own purpose or God's purpose for us. Many of us go through life on autopilot, mechanically doing the same things day after day. Does that sound familiar?

If you are genuinely honest with yourself, take a moment to reflect on these powerful questions: Do you know the life you truly wish to live? Do you understand your purpose and the reason for your creation? Are you aware of the dreams and desires you cherish but have yet to achieve?

We often become so overwhelmed by life and its challenges that we lose sight of what we truly want for ourselves. Years ago, I had a friend whose son, Ben, dreamed of joining the Air Force after graduation. He talked about the Air Force all the time. Everything he owned—his school backpack, his shirts, his jackets, and even most of his pants—reflected his passion for the Air Force and airplanes. This passion might have stemmed from his admiration for his father, who served in the Air Force and was his hero, or perhaps it was because his grandfather and several uncles also served in the military, inspiring Ben to follow in their footsteps. Or maybe it was simply his love for airplanes and the thrill he imagined experiencing while flying one.

Regardless, Ben's dedication was evident. He knew every step he needed to take to enroll, and he was prepared. A few months after graduation, Ben was set to head to the Air Force base to begin his journey. Every day, when the school bell rang at 3 PM, a group of friends would gather to walk to the train station together. About a month before graduation, as Ben was walking toward the station to head home for the weekend, the soon-to-be Air Force pilot gently tugged at his best friend Alisha's jacket, signaling that he wanted to talk privately. To her surprise, Ben looked troubled, as if he were on the verge of tears.

Linking her arm with his, Alisha looked into his eyes and gently asked, "What's wrong? Why do you look so sad?" A tear slipped down Ben's cheek, and in a soft, cracked voice, he replied, "I can't become an Air Force pilot anymore." More tears began to fall. Alisha was stunned, struggling to process his words. "Why are you saying that? What happened? What changed?" she asked. As she listened, a tear rolled down her cheek, sensing that something truly significant must have happened for him to give up on his dream.

She called out to the rest of the group, who were now several feet ahead, urging them to continue and take the train without them. Ben and Alisha would catch the next one so they could talk privately without interruptions. To her shock, Ben confided that he could no longer pursue his dream of becoming an Air Force pilot because he had just found out his girlfriend was pregnant. Alisha was stunned—she didn't even know he had a girlfriend, let alone that they were sexually active. He had never mentioned her to his friends, and she wasn't part of their usual group. His girlfriend had confided in her mother, who then informed Ben's parents, and just like that, his parents decided his dream was over.

If you're familiar with the Latino culture and the expectations of previous generations, you'll understand what happened next. In our culture, when a man gets a woman pregnant, he's expected to marry her and take responsibility for his "new family." Ben's parents insisted that he was to stay in Brooklyn, marry his girlfriend, and fulfill his new family obligations. They made decisions for him by telling him that the Air Force was no longer an option—his duty now was to care for his child. They expected him to find a job after graduation and support his new family.

In an instant, Ben's life changed completely. I'm sure he never intended this to happen, but life can take unexpected turns when we aren't careful or thinking clearly. Perhaps, in a fleeting moment, he became lost in the beauty of his girlfriend, the thrill of intimacy, or the rush of endorphins. Or maybe there were no thoughts at all—just a moment of desire, passion, lust, or love.

Regardless of the reason, there's no doubt that for a moment (or perhaps longer), Ben was distracted—and that distraction changed his life forever. Life will always distract us; it's inevitable in a world where we're constantly moving, busy, seeking, and striving to stay ahead. We live in a society that craves instant gratification, evidenced in K-cups, fast food, instant messaging, skip-the-line passes at theme parks, drive-throughs, minute rice, and curbside pickup—the quicker, the better. We often don't take the time to consider what we truly want: the places we wish to visit, the jobs we aspire to, and the partners we hope to share our lives with. We might not even think about what we want for dinner; instead, we drive through, grab something, bring it home, and call it a meal. It's convenient and easy, but it's also repetitive and doesn't bring joy, happiness, or peace. It's just another robotic move in our day-to-day living.

If any of this resonates with you, then you may not be exactly where you want to be. You might not feel pleased, and you may not even know what peace is, let alone possess it within yourself. Are you truly at peace with who you are, where you are, what you're doing, and with whom you share your life? Do you want to change that? Do you want to improve the life you're currently living? Do you want to make life happen for you, or will you allow life to continue to happen to you? Tony Robbins expresses it best: "You can choose for life to happen intentionally for you, rather than letting life happen to you." When you choose to live with intention, you control the life you create. However, when life happens to you, you accept whatever comes your way. So, how do you want to live your life?

A dear friend of mine, Jackie (a pseudonym for the book), once confided in me during a moment of vulnerability. She said, "I don't think I know what my purpose in life is." As a life coach, I often hear this;

many people share similar feelings and thoughts. At the time, Jackie was in her fifties and struggling in various areas of her life. She didn't have many close friends, and although she held a respected position in her industry, she no longer found joy in her work. She felt lost, unsure of her interests, uncertain about her passions, and disconnected from her own beliefs and values. She couldn't even identify what she loved to do.

Jackie once believed her purpose was her family. She loved them deeply and embraced the role of organizer and planner, arranging vacations, holidays, weekend getaways, and birthday parties—anything that brought everyone together. Jackie cherished creating these moments for her family, which included her husband and their two sons and two daughters.

As time passed, Jackie's children grew up and started their own lives. They went off to college, and two of them eventually got married and began families. With her children living in different states, Jackie and her husband, Bob, started to spend more time together, yet they still valued family gatherings during holidays and vacations. Jackie recognized that she needed to adjust her focus and expectations, so she redirected her energy into her marriage.

With them now being empty nesters, Jackie embraced the idea that her "new" purpose was to nurture her relationship with Bob and make the most out of their life together. She planned vacations, booked cruises, and reserved dinners at unique restaurants they had never tried. They were living the life they had always dreamed of. While occasionally visiting their grandchildren, Jackie and Bob spent most of their time together, savoring this new chapter.

Then, tragically and unexpectedly, Jackie's husband passed away, leaving her alone. One day, as we spoke, she looked at me with tear-filled eyes and said, "Sidrid, I don't know what my purpose in life is anymore. I thought my purpose was family, but then the kids grew up and left. I believed it was to share my life with my husband, but now he's gone. I feel so lost. I don't know what to do next. Can you help me rediscover myself? Can you help me find my will to live again?"

For those who don't know me, my purpose is to help people like Jackie—and to help you, too. My expertise lies in guiding individuals to achieve their goals, overcome obstacles, and reach their full God giving potential. I am passionate about assisting those who feel lost, confused, or need direction. My mission is to help you identify your strengths, weaknesses, and aspirations while providing the guidance, support, and accountability necessary to make meaningful progress personally, spiritually, emotionally, and professionally.

So, when Jackie asked if I could help her, my answer was a resounding YES!

Jackie was determined to rediscover her purpose and find happiness again. Together, we started working through my five-step process, beginning with identifying what she wanted to let go of—anything that no longer served her. This process helped Jackie find inner peace by releasing distractions, chaos, and the things causing disruption.

As we continued our work, we discovered that much of Jackie's inner turmoil came from self-limiting beliefs imposed by others. She had internalized the hurtful words people had said to her: "No one will want to be with you at your age," "You've already had your happiness; how dare you want more?" "What more do you want?" and "Just accept your life as it is now." These toxic statements replayed in her mind, weighing her down and stifling her hope. Our work together focused on releasing these influences so she could rediscover her true self, understand that she was worthy of more, and embrace the life she deserved.

Once Jackie decided to release these thoughts and distance herself from those who reinforced them, she began to discover activities she enjoyed and loved. We worked together to reshape her thinking, emotional responses, and belief patterns. Jackie soon recognized that she had been accepting aspects of her life that didn't align with her values and beliefs. Through her hard work, dedication, and commitment to the coaching process, Jackie experienced a breakthrough. With tears in her eyes, she looked at me and said, "I finally feel complete and know who I really am. I know what I want to do with my life, what makes me smile, and what I want to share with the world."

Her excitement was contagious, and I felt my own joy rising. At that moment, I realized Jackie had truly experienced her breakthrough. With tears streaming down her face, she looked at me, a radiant smile lighting up her face, and said, "I'm ready to live my new purpose. I'm ready to be myself. I love photography and traveling, so I will explore the world, take photos, and share them with anyone who wants to see them. I don't care who approves or criticizes—I will be true to myself. I might even get my photos into a gallery or exhibit one day."

My heart was overflowing with happiness for her. I had always believed this day would come, but I hadn't anticipated how profoundly joyful I would feel seeing her discover her new purpose and passion. Watching her embrace her vision of traveling, photographing, and pursuing her BHAG (Big Hairy Audacious Goal) of showcasing her work in a gallery or exhibit one day was incredibly fulfilling. I felt thrilled to witness her stepping into this new journey, and I am so grateful that she found what truly lit up her soul.

If you're searching for your purpose in life, start by identifying your passions—those things that get you out of bed each morning and make you feel alive. What do you love to do or dream of transforming into a career? What excites you and feels worth sharing with the world? As Steve Jobs famously said, "If you love what you do, you'll never work a day in your life." That's exactly what Jackie discovered.

Most people who understand their purpose actively live it. Here, the word "most" is crucial. They work tirelessly, often for hours or days without a break, but it doesn't feel like work—it feels like a mission, a passion, a desire to make an impact, leave a legacy, or empower those they encounter each day. They are fueled by their passion, using time effectively because, to them (and to us), time is valuable. We recognize the importance of utilizing time wisely to make a difference in our field of expertise. Our purpose, mission, and passion center around positively impacting and assisting others, ensuring that every moment counts.

Many people who fail to recognize their own worth often seem disconnected from themselves and perhaps even from their creator, the universe, or God. Their minds and lives are so filled with chaos that they feel too overwhelmed to take the time to discover their personal core values. Uncovering our core values requires intention; it demands a conscious desire to understand who we are and what we stand for. Without this understanding, we risk being unaware of what we can contribute to others or, even more importantly, our lives and the world.

When we fail to connect with our authentic selves, we can fall into a routine of simply going through the motions—living day by day without fully experiencing life's richness. We overlook opportunities to savor simple pleasures, like the scent of blooming flowers, the beauty of a sunrise or a sunset, or the joy of a date, a book, the warmth of your 1st cup of coffee every day, or setting new goals. When disconnected, we may miss the things that bring joy or purpose, such as visiting a dream destination, taking a salsa class, learning something new, attending church, or simply having fun. Life's possibilities are endless: building a snowman, starting a new hobby, getting a massage with friends, discovering chakra, trying meditation, adopting a pet, journaling, creating a vision board, or attending a wine-tasting class you've been curious about.

Recognizing our core values opens the door to a more meaningful and fulfilling life, where each moment presents an opportunity for joy, growth, and connection. When was the last time you wrote down your core values? When was the last time you looked in the mirror and saw your authentic self? In our busy lives, as we juggle countless tasks, it's easy to lose touch with who we are truly meant to be. And if you're a woman, that multitasking may feel like juggling hundreds of things all at once.

The gift of multitasking can become a burden when it causes us to lose sight of our core values, leading us to settle for whatever comes next. We accept what's in front of us or what's easiest because defining or revisiting our core values takes time—time that feels scarce or that we choose not to invest in. Amid the chaos of the world and of our own lives, we rarely pause to reflect on who we are, who we want to become, or what we genuinely desire. More importantly, we often overlook whether we are aligned with what our creator intends for us to be and accomplish.

Reconnecting with our core values paves the way for living a life of intention and fulfillment, while staying true to ourselves and our vision for life. Since you're already engaged with this book, in the next page take a moment to consider your core values. These values represent who you are today and can guide you toward becoming the person you aspire to be. Defining your core values brings clarity and ease to life.

Core values are the guiding principles that define what is meaningful to you; they help define who you want to be and help keep you true to yourself.. They shape your sense of right and wrong within your community, culture, and society. They establish a standard for behavior—qualities like patience, honesty, and integrity—that ultimately form your character.

Why not try this together? To begin, choose up to six values from the "Core Values" chart below that resonate most deeply with you. Please place them in the boxes provided, aiming for no more than six to ensure you focus on what truly matters.

My Core Values

Love	Courage	Humility
Kindness	Beauty	Happiness
Authenticity	Simplicity	Persistence
Playfulness	Achievement	Generosity
Integrity	Learning	Freedom
Purpose	Discipline	Honesty
Ambition	Faith	Compassion
Individuality	Respectfulness	Service
Enjoyment	Flexibility	Creativity
Community	Equality	Optimism

Understanding your core values enables you to make decisions with confidence and clarity. When your choices align with these values, you feel assured that you're following what you believe is right, paving the way for future happiness and better opportunities. They provide a sense of purpose and meaning and act as a compass when setting goals. Your core values also shape how you spend your time, where you invest your money, how you communicate, and even the places you choose to visit. For instance, if you value happiness and enjoyment, you might prioritize spending quality time with friends or engaging in activities that bring you joy.

Did you know that even God emphasizes the significance of core values? We are reminded of them as the "Fruit of the Spirit": love, joy, peace, forbearance, kindness, goodness, faithfulness, gentleness, and self-control. If faith is one of your core values, then staying connected with God, the universe, or a higher power is essential for you. Faith allows us to deepen this connection and draw strength from it.

For me, being connected to God is essential for navigating life's challenges. I recognize that not everyone shares this perspective, and I fully respect those with different values and beliefs. However, if you'll permit me, I'd like to explain why my faith is so important to me. When I connect with God, I gain a clearer understanding of my potential, increased confidence, and the realization that in the areas where I struggle or feel limited, my Creator provides a way. Doors open, opportunities arise, and I find clarity where I haven't seen it before. With faith as a core value, I'm assured that I can pursue the desires of my heart because they exist for a reason. I believe that God places these desires within us to guide us toward who we are meant to be, what we're called to do, and where we are destined to go. Through Him, I feel empowered to follow the path intended for me.

The more connected we become to God or a higher power, the more transparent our authentic selves are to us and others. This connection allows us to experience greater peace in all our lives. We begin to realize that what truly matters is seeing ourselves through the eyes of our creator, which helps us recognize and understand our worth. When we see ourselves as God sees us, we understand His love for us and the abundance He envisions in our lives. Through this connection, we can reflect on the person God created us to be, aligning His abundance with the desires of our hearts.

When we're align with our creator, we start to experience a deep and lasting sense of self-love, self-worth, confidence, and unconditional love for others, alongside building a stronger faith, experiencing true joy, peace, clarity, and acceptance. We cultivate a new mindset focused on what truly matters, which brings us happiness, fulfillment, protection, blessings, and a feeling of security.

I believe that discovering my true self through the perspective of my Creator has given me the freedom to be who I am, without worrying about those who may not appreciate my authenticity. I find peace in being the person God intended me to be. Through my relationship with God, I've also uncovered my passion for helping others, which has fostered a sense of confidence and strength, knowing that I can do all things without fear of others' opinions. Embracing my authenticity has become my protective armor, allowing me to live freely and fearlessly in alignment with God's purpose for my life. Isn't that something we all desire?

When we aren't connected to ourselves and our creator, our lives lack the depth and fulfillment our hearts truly desire. By "lack," I mean that every aspect of our lives and everyone is missing out. Whether it's family, work, or friends, no one gets to experience your true authenticity. Instead, they encounter a version of you: the fast, busy, trying-to-do-it-all you, the "I'm here right now, but not fully present" version of you. They aren't seeing the fully present mother, the engaged employee, or the genuine spouse or friend. What's missing for those around you is the gift of a truly connected and present you.

We often don't do this intentionally; most of us aren't even aware of it. Some might call it "just living life," but is it truly living if we're unclear about what we want from life or who we want to be? Ask yourself: If you're not honoring your true, authentic self, are you genuinely living the life you were meant to live? Are you embracing the life God created you for?

Discovering and developing the authentic person we were meant to be takes time. We need to create space to connect with our Creator, with God. And I say this gently: God may sometimes intervene and disrupt our plans if there's something we're called to do and we're too preoccupied to do it. You were created and chosen for greatness; there's no doubt that. There is a unique purpose for your life. If we're too distracted to connect with our Creator, He may halt us to ensure we can hear His guidance and pursue what we're meant to do. Let me share with you how my Creator guided me from where I was to where I am today, helping women discover their strengths, recognize their weaknesses, and guiding them to pursue their aspirations. Through this journey, I offer the support, and accountability needed to help them make meaningful progress personally, spiritually, and professionally.

I use to work for Corporate America at a medical billing company for ten years and loved my job. I built incredible relationships with my team, and we became the top-performing department in the region. My employees knew me well, understood our goals, were thoroughly trained, and respected my work ethic and authenticity. We genuinely enjoyed working together, and they valued being part of our team. My department consistently generated significant regional revenue, and our company's write-offs decreased by the thousands. There was mutual respect between employees and management, and everything ran smoothly for about seven years.

Then, unexpectedly, a significant shift took place. All the Senior Vice Presidents, Vice Presidents, Presidents, and several Regional Directors retired around the same time. The company was acquired, and a completely new management team assumed control. Suddenly, I went from loving my job to dreading it. My team, which had once looked forward to coming to work, began searching for jobs outside the company. The work environment became toxic almost overnight. The new management would curse at employees, belittle their work, and speak disrespectfully about them. This created a chaotic and unhealthy atmosphere. I remember coming home in tears many times, overwhelmed by the toxic environment that had replaced the workplace I once cherished.

Throughout the seven years of my career I had worked my way up to manager. However, as our finances strained, I started a side job from home that quickly grew into a successful business, generating a remarkable income for a "side hustle." It was fun, exciting, and a welcome escape from the chaos of my full-time job. I enjoyed the creativity and connection of social media, meeting new people, and simply being myself. What I loved most was sharing empowering messages at the end of my live sessions, where people's lives were genuinely touched and changed. My side business eventually became so successful that I was earning roughly the same amount as I did in my corporate job, though since it depended on sales, the income varied weekly.

Meanwhile, my full-time job became unbearable. The toxic environment worsened, and most days I returned home in tears. My team was frustrated and faced daily criticism from the new Director. The toxicity was contagious, spreading throughout the office and affecting everyone.

I prayed daily, seeking God's help because the negativity was impacting both me and my team. Then, one day, my husband looked at me and said, "You need to quit that job and focus on your side business. You're earning enough to do it full-time. Stop calling it a side hustle and recognize it for what it is—your business. I'll support you one hundred percent."

As I continued to pray, I knew I had to leave. I recognized it was the right decision, but I kept doubting myself. I knew He didn't want me in a place where I felt miserable. I noticed the toxic influence on my actions and responses. I found myself becoming angrier, and when my boss cursed at me, I would retaliate. It was unhealthy, even poisonous. I realized management wouldn't change, so I needed to change. I wanted to reclaim my inner peace and refuse to let anyone treat me disrespectfully. I am a strong believer that "people will always treat you how you allow them to treat you," and I wasn't going to tolerate the disrespect any longer. It was time to stand up for my team and myself. I needed to confront those toxic voices and forces at my job.

So I went home and wrote my resignation letter. I had my resignation letter tucked in my purse, ready to stand up for my values and confront those toxic individuals. I kept sensing that nudge in the pit of my stomach—an undeniable feeling that something (perhaps God) was urging me to act, to submit that letter, but I hesitated. I lacked the courage and confidence to follow through. My mind was filled with doubts: "What if I don't succeed in my business? What if I fail and can't replace the income from my full-time job? What if we can't pay the bills? What if we lose our homes or struggle with just one income? What if we encounter difficulties, and I can't find another job?" There were so many WHAT IFs.

I stayed with that toxic company, and over time, I became toxic myself. I was constantly angry and cursing—not just at them but in general. I even started to get frustrated with my team, which I had not done in a long time. My reactions reflected the negativity directed toward me. I felt mentally, emotionally, and physically drained. But fear held me back. I was scared that my "side hustle" wouldn't support us and that I couldn't replace the steady income I was earning from Corporate America.

In the end, I never resigned; instead, they fired me. Yes, they fired me in such a harsh manner that human resources marked my records to ensure I could never return to that company again. My file indicated that no department could offer me a position. Every part of me—my gut, my spirit, my God—was urging me to resign and leave on my terms, peacefully, with dignity and integrity, but I didn't listen. My fears overwhelmed me, leading me to engage in behaviors that ultimately closed the door on any chance of a transfer or future role within the company. I became exactly who they wanted me to be—angry, frustrated, resentful, humiliated, bitter, and hurt.

And that was certainly not who I, nor God, intended for me to become. I wasn't meant to revert to the unkind, unpleasant version of myself that had emerged during past heartaches. God wanted me—and wants all of us—to keep moving forward and let go of the past. But I wasn't listening to what I knew was right. I ignored my core values: respect and being respected, showing love and being loved, honesty, and integrity. I allowed my emotions to take control. Yet, even though I struggled, I can now see that God was still guiding my path, watching over me, and reminding me of who I was meant to be.

Whether we believe it or not, there's a silver lining to everything in life—if we choose to look for it and not dwell on the "what ifs." God had something bigger and better planned for me. By shifting my focus to my side hustle, I learned how to build my own business. After five years, that side hustle evolved into an enterprise, and today, I am the CEO and Founder of Sidrid Rivera Enterprises (SRE), a Life and Business Transformation Mindset Coaching company that empowers women to reach their full God-giving potential. We have grown to include a CFO and four administrative assistants, with plans to expand our team further. Over the past three years, we have coached hundreds of clients and launched three successful women's empowerment retreats, held numerous virtual seminars, webinars, and conducted monthly masterclasses. I have also written my first book (which you are currently reading) and I have already started writing my second book. In addition, I have had the privilege of speaking at multiple events, started my podcast called "Sip with Sidrid' where I inspire women to embrace their authentic selves.

I'm sharing this not to impress you, but to impress upon you that it is essential to listen to your gut, that nudge, or the Holy Spirit that leads you 99% of the time towards the right path. When you feel that nudge and stay true to your values and authenticity, God has incredible things in store for you. When fear tries to take over your mind and spirit, it often means that something greater is waiting for you, possibly right around the corner—something transformative that will bring you closer to the person you want to be. Looking back, I am grateful for being pushed off that ledge and out of a toxic job because it led me to a life filled with fulfillment, happiness, love, joy, peace, integrity, and true authenticity.

Some may wonder if I feel ashamed to admit that I was fired. My mom always told me, "Don't tell people you got fired; it's embarrassing, and it doesn't look good." I understand it might not seem ideal, but getting fired was one of the best things that ever happened to me. There's a story behind it. I was let go because God, our

Creator, had a bigger and better purpose for my life. I was created to help and serve others—people like you.

This experience taught me to pay close attention to the nudges in my gut and my spirit because that's how God connects with me—and perhaps with you, too. It's His way of guiding and protecting us. I once heard Jamie Kern Lima say, "Rejection is God's protection." What if being fired was God's way of shielding me from self-destruction? What if it were His method of ensuring I wouldn't return to that toxic environment or revert to the person I once was? What if this was His way of freeing me from that Corporate America job so I could focus on building my life coaching business, where lives are transformed? Maybe being fired was a way of setting me on the path to fulfilling my true purpose—helping others and impacting those who cross my path.

There was so much chaos and frustration in my mind and life that I couldn't think clearly. Have you ever felt that way? Have you ever been so overwhelmed that clarity seemed out of reach? Looking back, I realize that being fired was the rejection I needed for God's protection to guide me toward living my best life—the life I was meant to live. It's a life I love, focused on helping people, making an impact, and empowering people like you to reach the life you were designed to live.

\Being released from that J.O.B. (Just Over Broke job) reconnected me with God, bringing peace that ultimately led me to discover my purpose. Did you catch that? Let me repeat it: being freed from that J.O.B. reconnected me to God, which brought peace, and that peace revealed my purpose… YOU! My purpose is to help you, inspire and empower you, teach you how to discover your self-love and self-worth and support you in becoming the person you've longed to be. My purpose is to coach people just like you and me, drawing us closer to our authentic selves.

CHAPTER 4

BE YOU

"Don't trade your authenticity for approval. The world needs you to BE YOU."

"God needs you to BE YOU."

~ Sidrid Rivera ~

Do you know what's missing from your life? Are you aware of what you need to authentically BE YOU? If so, it's time to act. The hardest part is often understanding what's holding you back from being your true self. It takes time to figure out why you're not living authentically, but once you identify what's blocking you, commit to changing it.

Choose to **"BE YOU!"**

For me, it was the fear of financial instability—worrying about paying the bills, buying groceries, covering the mortgage, paying for gas, or managing unexpected expenses and not having the money.

Here's how to move forward:

1. Recognize Your Fear: Identify what is holding you back and develop a plan to overcome it.
2. Be Honest with Yourself: Don't pretend to be brave if you're struggling. God has your back. Cast your worries, anxieties, and fears onto Him, knowing you were chosen for greatness and that you are never alone.
3. Embrace Peace: Trust that God has a plan and align your plan with His. Life coaches can also help you discover inner peace.
4. Strengthen Your Connection with Your Creator: Nurture a deeper relationship with your creator. Meditate and spend time connecting spirit, mind, and soul.
5. Trust Your Instincts: Recognize that those inner feelings you are feeling can guide you toward the right path, if you let it.
6. Take Time to Discover Your Purpose: Identify your passion and work toward that goal. You have lives to impact and people to empower. How do you wish to achieve this?
7. Take Action: Trust the process, and let your true self shine.

If you're wondering how to change your mindset or how to move forward, let me tell you, it starts with a choice. Changing your perspective is a daily decision.

You must first choose to change, and once you do, it's like flipping a switch in your mind. You'll need to decide to think differently consciously. Tell yourself, I'm going to improve my life, my family, my career, and take steps to make that happen. Tell yourself, I'm going to live the life I deserve. This process involves positive affirmations, self-belief, and transforming your automatic thought patterns. When you decide to shift your mindset and fully embrace who you want to be, that's when transformation begins. Reconnecting with your creator can be an invaluable part of this journey.

Shifting your mindset involves embracing positive affirmations, fostering self-belief, and reshaping your automatic thought patterns, leading to an "I CAN" mentality. I reminded myself—and truly believed—that I could do all things through Christ who strengthens me (Philippians 4:13). Even when I didn't feel strong, I relied on God's strength to support me. By believing in myself and adopting an "I CAN" mindset I nurtured profound confidence and inner resilience.

I remember asking myself, "Why am I still working for Corporate America?" I'm educated, capable, genuine with people, and ready. I told myself, "I deserve everything God has in store for me. I deserve abundance, and I'm going to claim it." "I'm DUN"

— done working for others. I wanted to be my boss. Sometimes, we reach a season in life I call the "I'M DUN" season — it's the time when you are completely fed up with anything and everything that is holding you back. It's the moment when a switch flips, and your brain tells you it's time to conquer, it's time to become who you've always wanted to be, to live out who God intended you to be, and to pursue your desires without letting anything stand in your way. Even if you don't believe in a higher power, you too get that sense of readiness. It's that time when you know you are "DUN" with everything and everyone one and you are ready to DO U NOW!!

I believed that with God's help, protection, and guidance, I could inspire and empower people to become the best version of themselves; after all, I felt it in my gut. My mindset shifted every time I told myself repeatedly, "I CAN... I CAN do all things through Christ who gives me strength." The power in that statement filled me with the belief and strength I needed to become my true self. It empowered me to reach out to you. I knew that millions were living the lives they wanted—why not me? Why not you? I began to realize that I was the only one who could make my life happen, and so I did.

Have you reached a point where you're fed up with your current situation and ready to do more, and be more? If so, that's the moment you need to decide to make a change. It's the best time to choose to do things differently, to create the life you truly want. If I was able to do it, you could do it! It's the time when you decide to do you… to "BE YOU."

Some people plan their entire lives, and that's how they achieve their goals. But for many of us, it doesn't work that way. Many follow what they believe is right, only to realize years later that they're not truly happy. They become fed up with routine, tired of living a life that doesn't align with who they want to be or what they genuinely desire. And then, it hits them like a ton of bricks; they're finished with the BS. They assert, "I'm done not getting what I want, not being who I want to be, and not living the life I deserve. I'm done settling, staying in a hurtful marriage, enduring verbal, sexual, or physical abuse. I'm done with the cheating, the financial strain, the disrespect, and the health issues that hold me back. I'm done working hard and receiving no recognition. I'm done with the depression and the constant stress." When you reach that breaking point, you realize you are truly done "DUN done." It's when you understand it's time to "Do U Now." It's time to choose you. And when you choose to 'BE YOU' your mindset will begin to change, and when your mindset changes, your life changes, and that's when life truly begins.

That's precisely what happened to me. I looked hard at where I was, thought about what I wanted, and realized I was no longer willing to tolerate the BS. It was time for me to "Do U Now." It was time to focus on me! To choose me. To choose us (my husband and me), and it was time for you to choose you. When you finally choose yourself life is never the same. When you reach that point—the "I'm DUN" mindset point—your focus sharpens, and a powerful clarity sets in. Suddenly, you're laser-focused on who you want to become and what you want to achieve. This shift unleashes an indescribable energy and strength, igniting a fire within that drives you to pursue the desires of your heart: you actually live in a healthy relationship, you stand firm for your truth, values, beliefs, you come out to your family and friends, you change careers, you follow your passion, you go into ministry, you write your first book, and you attend the college you desire; you decide to search for your birth parents; you travel the world on your own; you go and have dinner at your favorite restaurant by yourself; or you loss all the baby fat that you've been unhappy with for years. You do things you wouldn't have done before.

This inner fire becomes so powerful that I feel unstoppable. I often tell my husband that my entire being is ablaze. I charge toward my goals with intensity, watching everything fall into place. My focus is undeniable, and I know with certainty what God wants me to do. My purpose is clear.

Most of us, however, have no idea what our true purpose is. We're raised with a basic blueprint: go to school, graduate from college, if possible, find a good partner, have kids, and work. If we're fortunate, we get to experience all of that. Yet, we are rarely encouraged to discover our unique, individual purpose. For older generations, purpose often meant raising children, building a stable marriage, and holding a steady job. Happiness was defined by paying the bills and, perhaps, taking a few vacations.

Previous generations didn't encourage us to think outside the box—not out of neglect, but simply because that was how they were raised. However, some of us, whom I call "different and daring," see the box and feel compelled to open it, exploring all it contains and more. We want to break free, discover the world, empower others, and build fulfilling lives. For those of us who are "different and daring," lifting the lid reveals a world that is larger, more vibrant, and infinitely more rewarding.

I'm one of those "different and daring" individuals. I noticed the lid, opened it, and jumped out, eager to explore a new world and share that experience with others. I want to help others do the same, realizing there's a more significant, brighter, more colorful life waiting beyond the one they're currently living.

You may be wondering, "Where do I begin? How do I start? What should I do first?" Three key areas come to mind:

1. God or Your Higher Power – Connect with God or your higher power. This connection will guide you toward your destined path and purpose.
2. Self Discovery – With God's guidance, direct your focus inward. Discover your true self, embrace your authenticity, and assess your reality.
3. Peace and Purpose—Connecting with your authentic self leads to peace. This inner peace serves as the foundation for your purpose.

Embrace these steps. When you put these principles into action God will guide you toward the desires of your heart. You also need to educate yourself and be honest with yourself. Here's the thing—you've got to "clean yourself up," which means looking within and working on being the best, most authentic version of yourself. Examine your life honestly and ask yourself: What must I change to become my best, true self?

Perhaps it's about truly believing in who you are. You can't tell others they're fabulous if you don't think you're fabulous yourself. You can't tell others you love them if you don't genuinely love yourself. You can't empower women's confidence if you lack confidence in yourself. You can't tell others that they are worthy if you don't believe you are worthy. Women will see right through that. You need to have faith in yourself, in who you are, in what you're saying, and in what you believe in if you want others to believe in you, too.

Continue to build on your strengths while acknowledging areas within yourself that require growth to fulfill your God-given purpose. If you lack authenticity, begin by being truthful with yourself. If you lack confidence, practice positive affirmations, establish personal goals, and nurture your physical, mental, and spiritual health. Clarity emerges when you prioritize self-care, and in doing so, you will uncover the next steps that will lead you to the life you were meant to live.

When it comes to being genuine, I have three tips I'd like to share with you:

1. Be genuinely authentic, not perfect. Perfection isn't the goal—it simply doesn't exist. God is the only perfect being. However, you can strive to be the person God intended you to be, making the most of what He has given you.
2. Don't fear what others think. It doesn't matter what they believe about you. What truly matters is what God thinks. Be unapologetically yourself, because you'll never please everyone. Focus on

pleasing God and let Him handle the rest. When you accept this, you'll find a profound peace in your heart.

3. Reflect on your purpose. Do you know what your purpose in life is? Have you thought about what God created you for? Each of us has a unique purpose, and it's our responsibility to discover it. What is your purpose in this world?

On the next page, take a moment to reflect on your purpose. If you're unsure, let's explore it together. Carry this book with you, and each time you feel excitement, joy, a sense of calling, or peace, write it down below. Mark this page so you know exactly where to return to capture those emotions. This is your time to either confirm or discover that you are on your path to living your authentic purpose. I can't wait to hear all about your journey.

Let's begin...

_____
_____
_____
_____
_____
_____
_____

CHAPTER 5

Where to Next?

"You can't really know where you are going until you know where you have been."

~ Maya Angelou ~

When you discover the real you—your purpose and values—you unlock a sense of peace in your heart and clarity in your mind. This inner clarity becomes your compass, guiding you toward the life you truly desire. You start to see where you are and where you want to go and you ask yourself, "where to next?"

This is the perfect moment to pause and reflect: What do I truly want out of life? What have I always dreamed of doing? Where have I envisioned going? What do I hope to accomplish?

Too often, we allow self-imposed boundaries to hold us back. Age, finances, circumstances, and education—or lack thereof—may seem like obstacles, but they don't have to define our limits. God opens doors where there seem to be none. What matters most is identifying what you want and pursuing it with intentionality and faith. When you invite God into your plans, the future can become much clearer.

So, if you're asking yourself, "What's next?" My answer is to begin by clarifying what you truly want from life. Every decision should align with your vision, bringing you closer to your goals. Unfortunately, many people struggle to feel fulfilled because they don't take the time to understand what they genuinely want. They live according to others' expectations or attempt to imitate others' lives, leaving them disconnected from their true self.

Real fulfillment starts with honesty—both with yourself and with others. To live the life you desire, you must first envision it clearly. As we discussed in the previous chapter, begin by identifying what truly brings you joy. Write down what matters most to you: the activities, experiences, and passions that excite you. What makes your heart sing? What sparks your passion? These reflections will shed light on the path to discovering the real you.

During my time in Corporate America, it didn't take long for me to realize that working under "bosses" who lacked the skills to perform my job was not for me. With over 20 years of experience in medical enrollment and billing, I was shocked when my company hired an unqualified Director and expected me to train her—teaching her everything about my role. If that wasn't disheartening enough, she became my boss. What the heck?! That was my wake-up call. I knew I needed to find my true passion and purpose because remaining in that environment wasn't an option.

While still working full-time, I started side-hustling in the evenings. I was laser-focused, energized, and determined to build something meaningful. Every day, I chipped away at my goals, fueled by the excitement of creating something new. Eventually, my side hustle evolved into a full-fledged opportunity, allowing me to leave Corporate America and embrace entrepreneurship. As an independent consultant, I discovered my passion: empowering women. Supporting others in making money, achieving their goals, and growing spiritually, physically, and financially brought me unparalleled joy. I became relentless in my mission to inspire and uplift others. The more lives I touched, the more fulfilled I felt, and my determination to make an impact only intensified. Through this journey, I discovered my purpose: becoming a life and business transformational mindset coach.

Once I discovered my true passion and purpose, I committed fully. Within a year, I launched Sidrid Rivera Enterprises (SRE), began coaching life and business clients, hosted a 12-week seminar series, ran monthly masterclasses, organized our first women's empowerment retreat with 18 incredible attendees from across the U.S., started a podcast, hired a team of currently six Administrators Coordinators, and began writing this book.

But this success didn't come easily. During that same year, I faced some of the toughest personal battles of my life: I was diagnosed with Type 2 diabetes and cirrhosis of the liver, navigated both Chapter 13 and Chapter 7 bankruptcies, supported my father through his fight with cancer, learned that my mother's husband had bladder cancer, and helped my mother through his passing, packed up my home without a clear plan for where we'd go, continuing to celebrate life's milestones such as birthdays, holidays, anniversaries and everything in between. These experiences shaped me, motivated me, and instilled in me the resilience to create a life I love. They remind me daily that purpose and passion aren't just words— they're the driving forces behind living a fulfilling and impactful life.

I never said that discovering your purpose and becoming the person, you are meant to be would be easy. On the contrary, stepping into who God created you to be takes hard work, perseverance, late nights, and resilience in the face of challenges. However, when you reach your potential—when you're living the life you've always dreamed of—you'll realize that every struggle was worth it. Embracing your authentic self—powerful, fearless, humble, and wise—is worth the effort. The journey of discovering your purpose and reaching your true potential is demanding, but its rewards are immeasurable.

To create the life we desire, we must start by evaluating what matters most. It's crucial to move beyond self-doubt, self-sabotage or believing we're unqualified or unequipped to achieve our dreams. Instead, we need to concentrate on what we truly want, whom we want to help, how we want to make a difference and trust that God will guide us. He has already equipped us with everything necessary to bring our vision to life. Ed Mylett says it best: "You are most qualified to help the person you used to be." But we have to take responsibility for our roles in our story. We must decide what we want to do and who we want to be. We are the lead characters in our lives, and no one else is responsible for our own happiness or success. It's up to us to take ownership of our choices and the direction we want our lives to take.

The dreams and desires stirring in our hearts are often seeds planted by God. When these desires persistently nudge us, it's not by chance—it's a call to pay attention and act. God's word reminds us: "Ask, and it will be given to you; seek, and you will find; knock, and the door will be opened to you." God invites us to bring these dreams to Him, to ask for His guidance, and to trust in His plan. He has the power to lead us and open doors we never knew existed, doors that align with the very opportunities and purposes He has placed within us. By trusting in Him, we can step boldly into the paths He has prepared, knowing He will provide what we need to bring those dreams to life.

When our desires align with God's plans, everything we believe we're lacking becomes attainable. The right people show up, finances come together, health and strength for the journey is restored—whatever we need, it's provided when we trust in Him. "Discovering what we want in life may lead us to uncover the purpose for which God created us."

I had nearly nothing to begin with—no experience, limited finances, and sometimes, not even the mental strength to write this book. Yet somehow, amidst the chaos—physical, mental, emotional, and financial—this book found its way to you. Call it what you wish; some may call it the universe; some may call it luck… I call it God. He made this book possible. Just when we feel like we lack what it takes to bring our passion and purpose to life, God intervenes and creates a path. Why? Because your dream, your passion, and your purpose are meant to create a difference. They are destined to assist someone, impact hundreds, transform a community, a village, a church—or even the world. God's purpose for us is to lead a life rooted in love and generosity, filled with meaning, goodness, faithfulness, compassion, and joy. Your purpose isn't solely for you; it's a gift intended to be shared with others, a way to reflect God's love and light through everything you do. The more you give of yourself—your kindness, your talent, and your passion-the more you will discover yourself blessed in return, often in ways that perfectly align with the desires of your heart.

Many of us have long understood what we're meant to do in life, yet we allow the noise, whether from our own doubts, family, friends, society, or even social media, to divert us. However, if that persistent nudge continues to touch your heart, there will come a time when you must stop ignoring it and take action. The longer you wait, the more intense the nudge becomes, until it's impossible to ignore.

Trust in yourself and in God to lead your life, not the expectations of others. Allowing others to dictate your path can steer you away from what God has planned for you, leaving you back at square one, questioning what you truly want. Remember: God will never tell someone else what He intends for your life. He speaks directly to you. That persistent nudge, that inner calling—that's His voice.

Tuning into the noise around you can distract you from the future that has been lovingly designed for you. If you let that happen, you alone will bear the consequences. Remember, God entrusted your life to you, not for others to dictate, but for you to embrace and follow the path He has specifically designed. It's not just about existing; it's about truly living the life you were created to fulfill. Trust Him, listen to His guidance, and boldly step into the purpose He has placed before you.

It's natural to seek advice from trusted people in your life but be careful not to let their views overshadow what God has placed on your heart. Stay focused on your desires and purpose—not the expectations of family, friends, or society. Don't sacrifice your unique path by losing sight of what truly matters to you.

Far too often, I've seen people abandon the life they were meant to live, choosing instead to please others. They end up feeling unfulfilled, drifting through life on autopilot. Even when fleeting happiness arrives, it never lasts. If you feel dissatisfied with your life or uncertain about your direction, it might be time to pause and reevaluate. Step back and reconnect with yourself and your higher power, who has already instilled the vision of your purpose within you. Life is a gift, and with it comes the power to choose how you live. Making choices that align with your heart, rather than the demands of others, leads to true happiness. You owe it to yourself to break free from the surrounding pressures and embrace the life God intended for you.

Happiness begins within, and when you choose yourself, it radiates outward. It isn't selfish; it's empowering. You are powerful, fearless, and capable of creating a life that reflects your identity. Others might not always agree with your decisions, and that's okay—it's your life, not theirs. During your season of reevaluation, seize the opportunity to draw closer to your creator. As the distractions fade, you'll gain clarity about His desires for you. Without the noise of external opinions, peace will follow, and you'll find the strength to live boldly in alignment with your divine purpose.

At the end of the day, when you walk in alignment with God's will and pursue the purpose He has placed in your heart, you will experience a life free from doubt, pain, and sadness. God never intended for us to seek the kind of love and fulfillment from others that only He can provide. Some people may feel uneasy or disapproving because you are not living according to their expectations; that is perfectly fine, you will feel liberated. I call this true freedom: the freedom to be yourself, to live authentically, and to embrace your identity as God's masterpiece. And that, my friend, is PRICELESS.

This clarity, peace, and freedom—the confidence to follow your calling because you are aligned with your higher power—is one of life's greatest gifts. You deserve to experience it. Living from God's perspective is transformational: He places you exactly where you need to be, helps you hear only what truly matters, and connects you with those who are meant to support your journey. In this divine alignment, the noise of negativity fades away. You're no longer distracted by voices that seek to diminish you and you're not surrounded by those who might hinder your progress. Instead, you stand protected, guarded, and empowered by your heavenly Father—your ultimate guide, your shield and source of strength.

To make better decisions for ourselves, it's essential to stay focused on what truly matters and seek prayer for guidance. God will always lead us toward choices that align with His life plan. Ensure your decisions bring you closer, not further away, from what you genuinely desire. Staying in alignment with God is the cornerstone of wise and purposeful decision-making. The world is full of opportunities—an abundant oyster waiting to be explored. By embracing its possibilities, we open ourselves to experiences and to the resources that will help us achieve our goals. Books, articles, webinars, podcasts, education, and thorough research are valuable tools to inform and refine our decisions.

Equally important are your values and beliefs, which serve as the foundation for authentic decision-making. Values reflect what matters most to you, and they never change. Take the time to write them down and revisit them as you choose your future. Whether it's integrity, hard work, faith, kindness, responsibility, or generosity, your values shape your life and keep you grounded in who you are. What truly matters to you? Is it freedom, independence, healthy living, love, prosperity, or faith? Perhaps it's the simple joys of life, such as enjoying an ice cream sundae, reading a book by a cozy fire, listening to Christmas music, or taking sunset walks with someone you love. Reflect on what aligns with your core beliefs—God, love, healing, equality, or moments of peace and joy. Your values act as a compass, guiding you toward decisions that resonate deeply within you and feel right for your soul. Remember, how you live reflects what you value most. Embrace this awareness, and let it lead you to a life filled with purpose, joy, and fulfillment.

Your values and beliefs define who you are. They offer a glimpse into your authentic self and form the basis for making meaningful decisions about your life. Google states, "A value in life is a belief or principle that guides how you live and work and helps you make decisions, act toward others, and measure your success. Values are an essential part of who you are, and they can help you live a more authentic life." Some of my core values and beliefs include my faith, integrity, freedom, independence, authenticity, gratitude, cherishing family and friends, being generous, loving others, empowering and inspiring women of all ages, enjoying good food and wine, marveling at sunsets, and always being fully present.

Understanding my values and beliefs has clarified what I will and won't accept in life. It helps me stay aligned with my purpose and grounded in what truly matters. With new people, daily decisions, and countless opportunities entering our lives, it's crucial to evaluate our surroundings and choices continually. This ensures we remain true to ourselves and stay connected to our purpose, happiness, and the path meant for us.

Remember, values and beliefs act as our compass, guiding us toward authenticity and fulfillment. However, it's our habits—the things we consistently do—that ultimately shape our lives. Are you living in alignment with your values and beliefs, or are you being shaped by habits influenced by life's experiences and others' expectations?

In the upcoming chapters, we'll discover what you truly desire for your life, what you want to explore, how you wish to contribute, and who you are ready to become. Let's explore this together. On the next page, take a moment to create a list of everything you desire in life—no holding back. Write down every goal, dream, and aspiration, whether big or small. Don't worry about what you currently have or don't have; this is a space for your imagination and heart to roam freely. Once you have written your desires, list your core values and beliefs. This simple exercise will be the first step toward becoming the person you've always envisioned. Let's begin the journey to uncover the life you are meant to live.

My Desires:
(List below your every hearts desire. There are no limitations. This is your space to finally write down everything you've ever wanted, so just do it.)

My Values:
(What's most important to you. Ex: Loyalty, Honesty, Love, Wealth, Freedom, Family, Success, Spirituality)

My Belief:
(Ideas you hold to be true. Ex: Generosity, Authenticity, Appreciation, Compassion, Courage, Beauty.)

CHAPTER 6

Pray About It

"Therefore I tell you, whatever you ask in prayer, believe that you will receive it, and it will be yours."

~ Mark 11:24 ~

In December 2007, the Great Recession began, though there was nothing "great" about it. It lasted until June 2009, with 2008 being a tough year for many, including my husband and I. For the first time, we found ourselves truly struggling financially. Despite both of us working full-time jobs and earning extra income from side businesses, our combined efforts still weren't enough to cover all our monthly bills.

In December 2007, the Great Recession began, though there was nothing "great" about it. It lasted until June 2009, with 2008 being a tough year for many, including my husband and I. For the first time, we found ourselves truly struggling financially. Despite both of us working full-time jobs and earning extra income from side businesses, our combined efforts still weren't enough to cover all our monthly bills. I'll never forget the day my husband called me to share some difficult news: we were about a thousand dollars short of our mortgage payment. We worked long hours, doing everything possible to make extra money, but it still wasn't enough. We had no idea where the extra thousand dollars would come from, and asking for help wasn't an option—everyone around us was struggling, too.

So, what do you do when your hands are tied, and there seems to be no way out? What did we do when we had exhausted all options? We prayed. I turned to Ricky and said, "When we bought this house, we knew it was meant to be our home. You found it, and the previous owner specifically wanted you—us—to live here. God placed us in this home, and He will provide for us now, just as He did back then. We need to pray and ask Him to open the heavens and help us this month and every month thereafter." And so we prayed about it.

We prayed with faith, persistence, and the belief that God would provide. Then, just two days before the first of the month, we received an unexpected letter from our insurance agency. The letter explained that one of their clients had won a lawsuit, and as a result, everyone with a similar policy would receive a portion of the settlement. Enclosed was a check for, guess how much? One thousand dollars. Yes, exactly one thousand dollars—the exact amount we needed, the precise amount we had been praying for.

Naturally, our first reaction was, "Is this real or just a scam?" So, we called our insurance agent, explained the letter and the check, and he confirmed that the check was a legitimate check. The check was genuine, and we could safely cash it. So, we did—and our mortgage was paid, and it was paid on time. Call it coincidence, luck, or whatever you want, but my husband and I knew God had heard and answered our prayers.

While we waited for an answer, a miracle, the experience only strengthened our faith. Think about it—how often does someone receive an unexpected check for a thousand dollars from a lawsuit they didn't even know existed, simply because they happened to have the same type of policy? That doesn't just occur. To us, it was nothing short of a miracle from God.

Prayer is essential for building a strong foundation with God. It brings hope when hope seems lost and reassures us that there is someone greater than ourselves who can make the impossible possible. Through prayer, we discover what we truly want, who we are meant to be, and how to align with our higher purpose. Prayer connects us with God—our guiding force—and leads us to live authentically. It's the key to understanding the true desires of our hearts, providing clarity, peace, and direction. When we pray, we create space for stillness, allowing us to reflect deeply on what matters most. Prayer centers and grounds our spirit, helping us navigate life's chaos with focus and intention.

Sometimes, my world feels overwhelming; my mind is cluttered, and everything seems out of place. I find myself wanting to disappear or flee far away. Ever felt that way? I'm sure we all have at some point. In those moments, I turn to prayer. Prayer is can be anchor—the one thing that helps us recenter, restores our clarity, and reconnects with our purpose. It quiets the noise that at times causes us to fall apart, leaving no room for procrastination or fear. Prayer reminds us of who we are and what we are created for, reigniting our focus on the goals and dreams God has placed in our hearts. It reassures us of this truth: that we "can do all things through Christ who gives us strength." It gives us the courage to move forward, persevere, and stand firm during life's challenges. It soothes our soul, cleanses our mind, restores our spirit and renews our vision. Prayer is more than a practice—it's a lifeline. It sustains our spirit, strengthens and connects us to our Creator, and brings us back when we feel distant or defeated.

This gift is available to all of us. Through prayer, you can reconnect with your true self and receive support for your goals. Prayer can provide the strength to overcome daily challenges, move forward, and fulfill the desires of your heart. Prayer will empower you to persist through life's obstacles and remain steadfast in your values and beliefs. Prayer calms the soul, clears the mind, and sharpens your vision, guiding you to see your desired path and the life God has planned for you. But how do you begin to pray if you've never donut or if you haven't done it in a long time? Let me assure you—it's easier than you may think.

In my faith tradition, praying to God is simply about talking to Him. Open your heart and share whatever you're feeling. Tell Him everything—your hopes, fears, doubts, and even the things you're hesitant to express. Be fully present with Him. There's no single "correct" way to pray; it's just a conversation between you and God, as natural as speaking to a close friend or trusted confidant. Share your feelings, thoughts, desires, dislikes, dreams, and needs. Prayer is a beautiful and intimate way to connect with your higher power. Jesus said, "But when you pray, go into your room, close the door, and pray to your Father, who is unseen. Then your Father, who sees what is done in secret, will reward you" (Matthew 6:6).

To start praying, simply open your mouth and speak. Begin with something like, "Hey God, it's me, [your name]. I just wanted to talk to you about…" and let the words flow. There's no perfect formula—just speak from your heart. You can talk to God anytime, anywhere about anything. However, I recommend starting your day with prayer. Scheduling prayer in the morning can set a positive focused tone for the day ahead. Beginning your day with prayer empowers and equips you to face life's challenges with a renewed mindset and strengthens your connection with God. Daily conversations with God are incredibly impactful. Instead of waiting for a crisis, start talking to Him regularly. It transforms not only how you approach your day, how you react to unexpected circumstances, and it builds your relationship with God and with others. Prayer is a gift, a lifeline, and an ongoing conversation that connects you to the One who knows you best. Don't hesitate—start talking to Him today.

Alongside prayer, worship serves as a powerful practice, and it can take many forms. My two favorites are (1) spiritual meditation and (2) praise and worship singing. Spiritual meditation is about discovering a quiet space, just you and God, where you can reflect and deeply contemplate. For me, praise and worship singing involves singing along with a Christian worship song, allowing the music and lyrics to connect me more deeply to God. I cherish closing my eyes, stilling my mind, and simply being present in the moment, taking deep breaths, and listening to the words of a beautiful Christian worship song.

Sometimes, I join in singing, and other times, I let the lyrics wash over me, letting them seep into my heart and soul. Worship, for me, is about a profoundly personal connection with God that I can only experience with Him.

When you worship, let your mind go, don't think about anything. Be open to feeling and hearing the song's lyrics with your heart and spirit. I'd like you to try this exercise with me so you can truly experience what worship feels like.

Please read this section first and carefully before doing the exercise:

* Visit YouTube and look up "Leeland - Way Maker (Official Live Video)."
* Play the video, and while the music plays, close your eyes and listen to the lyrics. Let the words sink into your heart, mind, and soul.
* As the song plays, release all your struggles, challenges, addictions, depression, loneliness, broken relationships, fears, self-doubt, feelings of unworthiness, financial worries, or any other burdens you are currently facing. Just let them go; surrender them to God. In other words, let go and allow God to take those from you.
* While listening to the song be sure to focus on the chorus part, it starts with the word "Waymaker."

> Listen to the chorus and let the words penetrate into your heart.

* And once again, release those emotions that you have been carrying for a long time to your creator, the one who can help you overcome all adversity.
* Don't be surprised if you experience goosebumps or shed a few tears. That's the beauty of worship; it's the power of connecting to God through worship music.

The beauty of praise & worship is that you can engage in it every day, multiple times a day: while driving, while in the shower, at church, taking a walk, cleaning, washing dishes, in your backyard, at home—anywhere you choose—because worshiping God is simply an expression of your love for Him.

Prayer is not something you have to do alone. There is great power in praying with others. In Matthew 18:20, God's Word reminds us, "For where two or three are gathered together in My name, I am there in the midst of them." God delights when we come together, especially in prayer. Praying with others builds confidence, strengthens belief, and deepens faith. It's a powerful way to create unique bonds and foster brotherhood or sisterhood.

I love praying with my friends. There's immense comfort in knowing that someone is agreeing with me in prayer. Romans 15:30 reinforces this truth: "I urge you, brothers and sisters, by our Lord Jesus Christ and by the love of the Spirit, to join me in my struggle by praying to God for me." God didn't design us to face life alone. He calls us to support one another in prayer, uplifting and growing stronger together as we navigate life's challenges.

There has been countless times when I've called my friends, or they've called me seeking prayer during difficult moments. We often see requests from people all over social media asking for prayers. The experience of praying together brings a profound sense of love, unity, peace, and victory. There's nothing like the power of united prayer among believers.

In August 2023, Sidrid Rivera Enterprises hosted our first Women's Empowerment Retreat, "What's Life About… YOU." This four-day, three-night retreat brought together a number of remarkable women to share their life experiences, faith, and journeys of transformation. It was an unforgettable event filled with love, laughter, and meaningful connections.

During those days, we learned so much about each other—our families, jobs, struggles, faith, triumphs, and dreams. The women shared what they needed to let go of and embraced the beauty of prayer and supporting each other. Witnessing them pray together, encouraging one another, and forming unbreakable bonds was genuinely inspiring. One of the most impactful moments occurred on the final night of the retreat, where I guide the women through an exercise of a personal letter they wrote throughout the retreat, to either God, or themselves or to someone they wanted to forgive. In these letters, they poured out their hearts, releasing burdens they no longer wished to carry and committing to a fresh start. Some expressed gratitude, others shared their struggles, and all embraced the chance for renewal.

Afterward, we burned those letters as a symbolic act of surrender and transformation. The feedback was unanimous: this exercise was life changing. The women described it as the most powerful, empowering, and refreshing moment they had ever experienced. Prayer brought us together during that retreat in ways that words can barely express. It showcased the remarkable power of faith, the beauty of sisterhood, and the profound experience of uniting before God.

How does prayer resonate with you when you read about it in this chapter? Is it a new concept, or is it something you're already familiar with? If you had the opportunity to write a prayer and share your thoughts, feeling, and emotions what would your prayer convey? In the following page take a moment to write your own prayer. Let God know what your thoughts are, what your feelings are, what you are needing, desiring, and longing for. This is your time to unite or reunite yourself with your higher power.

Dear Heavenly Father:

_____
_____
_____
_____
_____
_____
_____
_____
_____
_____
_____
_____
_____
_____
_____
_____
_____
_____
_____
_____
_____
_____
_____
_____
_____
_____
_____

Note to Reader: For additional templates visit my website https://sidridrivera.com/resources or scan QR Code.

CHAPTER 7

I AM

"I am who I am. Not who you think I am. Not who you want me to be. I am me."

~ Brigitte Nicole ~

What do you say when someone asks you, "Who are you? or Tell me a little bit about yourself." Have you been stuck not knowing how to respond? How would you respond to the two most powerful words in the English language: "I AM..."?

For many, answering this question can be quite challenging. It may require digging deep and uncovering truths about themselves that they haven't fully explored. Or perhaps they don't know how to define themselves beyond the surface.

Take a moment and try it—go ahead and finish the phrase: "I AM..."

What comes to mind?

I AM...

_____
_____
_____
_____
_____
_____
_____
_____
_____
_____
_____
_____

I remember when someone first asked me, "Who are you?" I was startled I froze for what felt like an eternity. It struck me as such a profound question, and yet, at that moment, I wasn't sure how to answer it. Of course, I believed I knew who I was; it's easy to provide a surface-level response: "My name is Sidrid Rivera. I'm an entrepreneur, I think I was 40 years old at the time, and I'm happily married to Ricardo Rivera." Sounds simple and straight forward, right?

If I were to ask you the same question, wouldn't your answer likely be similar; simple and basic, right? Yet, reflecting on this question, I realized something profound: Who I am isn't just about the basics. It's not solely about our age, our marital status, or the titles we hold in my business or in life. Who we are goes far deeper than those surface-level facts. "I AM..." is internal; it's the essence of what makes us the woman or man we are today.

As I kept pondering, I realized that our identity is influenced by our beliefs, values, life experiences, and the choices we've made despite those experiences. "I AM..." is about who we decide to be each day.

Let me explain this with the baking a cake metaphor. Have you ever baked a cake? I haven't baked one myself—I'm not much of a baker—but I loved watching my mom bake when I was a little girl. I remember how she'd mix all the ingredients: flour, sugar, eggs, and whatever else went into her recipe. She'd whisk everything together until it became a smooth batter. Then she'd pour it into the baking pan, leaving just enough behind for me to scrape the bowl clean—it was like when eating raw cookie dough, delicious. I would beg her to leave some batter on the spoon for me, savoring every lick. Once the batter was placed into the oven the cake would transform into something beautiful and incredibly delicious. However, all those ingredients by themselves would not much to admire and most likely would not taste just as delicious as when they are all put together.

The journey of becoming who we are can resemble baking a cake. It's about how all the ingredients of our lives—our experiences, struggles, joys, and choices—come together to create something unique and extraordinary. A single ingredient, such as our title or age, doesn't define our identity. It's the blend of everything, mixed and refined, that shapes who we truly are. Uncovering who you are is much like baking a cake. Just as a cake requires key ingredients, your life needs essential elements to shape who you become. Without the right ingredients, the cake simply can't come together. If the ingredients are off, the cake might taste terrible, look like a disaster, or even fall apart.

The same holds for life—if you don't know who you are or lack the right "ingredients," your life can feel chaotic and unstable. Just as baking demands precision and care, becoming the person you aspire to be involves identifying and nurturing the key elements that make you whole. Regardless of the type of cake you want to bake, most cakes share a common set of ingredients: flour, baking powder, baking soda, butter, milk, sugar, egg whites, vanilla extract, and possibly frosting or fondant for decoration. What makes your cake unique, however, isn't just the ingredients—the time, care, and love you invest in creating it.

Similarly, what makes you unique isn't just the foundational elements of your life, such as your background, experiences, or values. It's how you choose to invest in yourself, how you nurture your passions, and how you embrace the process of becoming the person you were meant to be. Your personal "recipe" reflects your dedication and the love you pour into your journey of self-discovery and growth.

I believe it's essential to understand the key ingredients—or key elements—that shape who you are. These include your experiences, expectations, beliefs, values, and perceptions about life. By truly grasping these components, you can assess whether the person you are today aligns with the individual you wish to become tomorrow.

Self-discovery is essential because it allows you to avoid being shaped by the opinions and expectations of others. Too often, we allow other people's ideas about who we should be to dictate our choices. But as I frequently remind my friends when they're worried about others' opinions: "What other people think about you is none of your business." Why? Because no matter what you do, you will never please everyone. Instead, you should focus on choosing to become the person you aspire to be.

We cannot let others influence or define who we should become. That role is reserved for God and us. When you allow others to "add their ingredients" (yes, I had to go there again) to your life, you lose your authenticity, both with yourself and with others. Letting others dictate your identity is like permitting someone else to mix their ingredients into your cake. Consider this: would that still be your cake? Would it genuinely reflect who you are? No. You risk becoming a version of yourself shaped by others' expectations instead of your authentic self. As my wise book coach, Jim Connolly, told me once: "You must know the ingredients that make you, YOU."

It's incredibly important to choose who you become. Do you know your values and beliefs? Understanding who you are is the foundation for becoming who you want to be. Yet, too often, people feel entitled to voice opinions about who we should be, and if we let their input influence us, it can alter the desires of our hearts—or worse, steer us off the path you were created for. This is why so many people feel lost in life: they stray from their true purpose because they are constantly listening to others instead of tuning into themselves and the nudges placed in their hearts. Those nudges are intentional—they guide us to live the life that is intended for us. However, if you're constantly absorbing what others think or say about your life, we risk living confused and full of clutter in our minds. Confusion leads to indecision, leaving us stuck and disconnected from what we are meant to do and accomplish in life.

You can't allow the noise in your mind to dictate your decisions. Instead, concentrate on what God has planned for you and what your heart truly desires. While it's fine to listen to others' opinions, especially from those who genuinely care about your best interests, your ultimate decisions should align with what God has placed in your heart and the truth found in His Word.

I once asked an essential question during one of my Masterclass sessions on decision-making: "Are you making most of your decisions with your heart or your mind?" In other words, are you decisions being made because of how you feel, on the emotions you're experiencing at the time of making a decision; or are you taking the time to think about what your decision needs to be? The women participating in the masterclass training paused to reflect, and their answer surprised even themselves: they were all making emotional decisions.

The decision-making process involves evaluating both attitudes and actions. Decisions are acts of the will, influenced by both heart and mind. However, it's crucial to remember this: the choices we make ultimately reflect the desires of our hearts. When we decide with our hearts, we are often guided by emotion. But is relying solely on our feelings the best approach? Emotional decision-making can sometimes cloud our judgment, leading to impulsive choices that we may later regret. While emotions are valid and significant in our lives, it's important to balance them with thoughtful consideration, wisdom, and prayer.

When you focus on what you honestly want and allow God to guide you, you will make the right choices for your life. As Proverbs 19:21 states, "Many are the plans in a person's heart, but it is the Lord's purpose that prevails." This is a powerful reminder that God's purpose will always lead us toward what we were created for. Luke 22:42 reinforces this truth: "Not my will, Lord, but your will be done." Living in alignment with God's will brings joy, fulfillment, and the abundant life He desires for us, ultimately allowing us to live the life we want. By trusting His guidance, you will find yourself walking the path to your most significant purpose.

If you want to be confident in your decisions, ask yourself this crucial question: "Am I choosing to please myself, or am I choosing to please the Lord with the decision I am about to make?" This simple reflection can help you determine whether you are being authentically true to yourself and aligned with God's purpose—or if you are being influenced by what others think you should do.

Essentially, knowing yourself is the foundation of being yourself, enabling you to love yourself and the life you're living. When you truly understand who you are, you gain clarity about what you need to do and the path you're meant to follow. This connection to your purpose helps keep distractions at bay. By remaining grounded in your identity and purpose, you can make decisions that honor both yourself and God.

As you discover who you are, it's crucial to avoid distractions. You cannot let the thoughts, opinions, beliefs, or behaviors of others, or even your surroundings deter you. Allowing distractions can prevent you from reaching your destination or fulfilling your destiny. Distractions derail you from your purpose, keeping you from becoming the person you're meant to be, going where you're supposed to go, or achieving what you're destined to accomplish.

To stay on course, you need a plan, a pathway, and a clear focus on who you want to become and where you want to go. It's like using a GPS. A GPS, or Global Positioning System, is a 24-satellite navigation system that uses signals to pinpoint a receiver's location on Earth, enabling you to travel from one place to your desired destination promptly. When driving to an unfamiliar area, most of us depend on our GPS to guide us, ensuring we don't get lost and helping us arrive on time.

Likewise, in life, we need our own "GPS." I refer to it as God's Pathway System. Just like a GPS finds the best route to your destination, God's Pathway System guides your spiritual journey, directing you toward the life He has crafted for you. When challenges or detours appear, God's Pathway System recalibrates, presenting alternate routes that still lead to His purpose for your life. Even if you take a wrong turn, His grace redirects you, ensuring you're never truly lost.

The "map" is His Word, the "signal" is the Holy Spirit, and the "destination" is living in alignment with His will. With faith as your compass and trust as your fuel, God's Pathway System guides you step by step toward the abundant life you desire and He promises.

A significant part of discovering who you have come from life's experiences and how you reflect on and learn from them—essentially reverse engineering your life. Let me illustrate with an example. One Saturday evening, my husband and I went to a restaurant for dinner. He ordered a ribeye steak, one of his favorite dishes, and was eagerly looking forward to it. However, when the steak arrived, it didn't meet his expectations. After taking a few bites, he appeared disappointed. I asked him, "What's wrong? Aren't you enjoying your steak?" He replied, "It's not what

I expected. It needs more salt, some grilled onions, and garlic butter." After a few more bites, he decided not to finish it. I suggested he take it home, and I promised to make him steak and eggs for breakfast the next day, seasoning it exactly how he wanted. The next morning, I made steak and eggs with grilled onions, garlic butter, and a tad bit of salt. When he took his first bite, he smiled and said, "Baby, this is delicious! Exactly how I wanted it." We jokingly say I 'Ricktified the steak'—since his name is Ricky— instead of rectified! This illustrates an important point: sometimes, to align things with what you truly want, you need to adjust, refine, or "Ricktify" them to match your vision. Similarly, in life, we must modify and fine-tune our paths to align with our desires, God's plan and our authentic selves.

This is a great example of how you can reverse engineer your life. If you feel like you're missing some "key ingredients" to create the life you desire, go ahead and Ricktify it (yes, you can borrow this new word—LOL). Use your GPS (God's Pathway System) to evaluate where you are, determine where you truly want to go and make the necessary changes to become the person you're meant to be. Ask God for guidance, and He will deliver—Matthew 7:7 reminds us: "Ask, and it will be given to you."

Take a moment to assess what isn't working in your life and chart a new course. You can redirect your journey, concentrating on the person you wish to become, and the purpose God has placed in your heart.

Here are three key ingredients that helped me uncover my purpose, and focus on my life's path. These same ingredients can help you as well:

1. **Believe in Yourself:** I use to struggle with believing in myself. I feared what others would say about me—whether they would doubt or question my abilities. That fear held me back from pursuing many opportunities. I constantly asked myself questions like, "Should I?" or "What if I fail?" Sometimes, I thought, "Maybe… or maybe not." Looking back, I realize my lack of belief wasn't about my family didn't believe in me; it was my internal and personal thoughts and feelings. No one was holding me back but me. For example, I almost didn't attend college because I was afraid people would say I wasn't smart or good enough. I was never told that I simply thought that because I didn't know many people in my community who actually went to college, who got a Masters degree or who was a lawyer, doctor, or a professional success.

   Believing in ourselves is a lifelong struggle because

it's rooted in our mindset. Even now, as I write this book, I grapple with self-doubt. There are moments when I would sit in my kitchen and wonder: Should I be doing this? Is this the right choice? Am I wasting my time? Will anyone care? Why would anyone want to hear from me? These questions creep in, especially since I don't personally know any authors (except for my coach and his wife). But here's the truth: it's ALL about our mindset. The real battle isn't about our abilities or potential—it's about whether we let doubt derail our journey, our path, and our life goals.

Let me be clear: it wasn't that I doubted my potential or passion. I trusted the nudge God placed in my heart and I know He could use me to help others and make a difference in their lives. My hesitation came from not knowing anyone who had accomplished what I was attempting to do. I didn't know there are people out there that do need to hear what is write-in this book. I didn't know many people who had dreams and actually became the person they aspired to be. So naturally, I questioned: Am I different enough to make this happen? Can I do it when so many others haven't?

There will be times in your life when people won't love the #RealYou. As I mentioned earlier, that's none of your business, that shouldn't matter to you any longer. You need to reach that point where other peoples opinions no longer hold power over you. We don't live to please others—we live to please God, to be true to ourselves, and to love one another. God is the One we must prioritize. When we seek to please Him, He blesses us with the desires of our hearts. Psalms 37:3-4 say it beautify, "Trust in the Lord and do good; dwell in the land and enjoy safe pasture. Take delight in the Lord, and He will give you the desires of your heart."

The truth is, there will always be people who don't like or support the "new you," and that's not your burden to carry—it's theirs. As long as you stay true to your purpose and God's plan for your life, He will take care of anyone who tries to derail or destroy you. Yes, some may actively work against you, but don't worry God handles those unkind, ugly individuals. Has I have said numerous times... "God don't like ugly spirited people." You won't always be everyone's favorite, and that's perfectly fine. Once you accept this, you'll discover a great deal of freedom, peace and joy. You'll no longer waste energy trying to win over those who don't believe in you or aren't meant to be part of your journey. Focus on pleasing God and living in line with your purpose—everything else will fall into place.

2. **Get Closer to God:** This was the key ingredient in creating my desired life. It was essential for achiev-

ing my goals, including some truly ambitious ones. I began to pray more and delve deeper into God's Word. I prayed for Him to remove my fears and draw me closer to Him and His plans for my life. Whenever negative thoughts entered my mind, I replaced them with empowering scripture or played praise and worship music to shift my focus. I did whatever it took to counter the negativity and realign my thoughts with God's truth.

One of the acronyms for FEAR is False Evidence Appearing Real. Fear is often nothing more than an illusion we create in our minds. When you learn to control those thoughts and rest in God's Word, fear begins to lose its grip. As 2 Timothy 1:7 reminds us, "For God gave us a spirit not of fear but of power and love and self-control."

Today, I feel closer to God than ever before, but this connection didn't happen overnight. It took practice, dedication, and a transformational shift in my mindset. I had to stop doubting myself and my abilities. I leaned on verses like Philippians 4:13, which says, "I can do all things through Christ who strengthens me." This scripture, along with others, gave me the confidence to stop worrying about what others thought of me. I ceased fearing the future and wasting energy on people's opinions. Instead, I focused on staying aligned with God's Word and making decisions that honored Him.

Certainly, someone will always find a reason to be offended, but I no longer let that disturb me. My book, my business, my life, and business transformational coaching, my seminars, and my spiritual retreats are all centered on God's Word and His message. I trust God to care for anyone who has an issue with what I do. When you reach a point where you're no longer afraid of criticism, that's when you have truly ARRIVED. That's the moment you've become the person God intended for you to be.

Here's what's incredible: I never had a family member tell me I couldn't do something. No one ever shattered my dreams or outright discouraged me. It was me—I sabotaged myself. I assumed others wouldn't approve of my ideas, dreams, or desires. I spent so much time worrying about disapproval that I allowed it to hold me back, even though that disapproval never actually came—at least not from those who mattered.

My mom sometimes questioned how I would manage certain things, like going to college, especially since we lived paycheck to paycheck. But she never outright told me I couldn't pursue it. If I devised a plan, she would say, "Aya tú," which means, "It's up to you" in Spanish. My parents didn't have the means to financially support me. However, they never discouraged me from attending college because we couldn't afford it. The barriers were in my mind, not theirs. Once my mom said, 'It's up to you,' I took full responsibility. I worked hard to secure scholarships and juggled multiple jobs to cover my tuition and other expenses. I made sure I made it happen.

If you are someone who has felt doubted, dismissed, or overlooked—this is for you. You may have had people who couldn't see your potential, who questioned your dreams, or made you feel like you weren't enough. But let me remind you: their inability to believe in you has nothing to do with your God-given purpose. You were not created for their approval—you were created to rise, to impact, to become everything God has already declared over your life. Even if no one claps for you, keep showing up. Even if no one sees your worth right now, keep being you. You don't need a crowd's validation to walk in your calling—you just need faith, courage, and the willingness to believe in yourself the way God believes in you. One day, the very people who couldn't see you, will witness the woman God always knew you would become.

3. **Discover Your Passion** — Discovering my passion meant erasing my doubts and fears. I realized that fear was holding me back from becoming the person I was meant to be, so I made the choice to stop

being afraid. Instead of letting fear control me, I chose faith over fear and transformed my fear into the fuel for my passion.

When I decided to let go of fear and concentrate on what I loved and what I was meant to do, I finally experienced a profound sense of fulfillment. It was at that moment that I realized my passion was perfectly aligned with God's purpose for my life, and I have never been happier.

This realization didn't happen overnight. It required reprogramming my mind to stop entertaining negative thoughts and to start acting. Every time a negative thought would creep in, telling me I couldn't succeed, I would tell it, "I can do all things through Christ who strengthens me" (Philippians 4:13). I didn't just whisper it—I repeated it louder and louder until I believed it. And if it wasn't that biblical promise I would yell out loud another one until I believed that one as well.

Finding your passion involves discovering happiness in yourself and what you do. Unfortunately, many individuals never attain that level of happiness because they focus too much on the opinions, feelings, words, or beliefs of others. Is now your time to discover what your words will be after "I AM…"? Ask yourself: AM I ready to live the life

I was designed to live? AM I ready to pursue my dreams? AM going to believe in me, my plans, and in my purpose? Is it time for you to BE YOU?

You need to live your life for YOU. There will always be people trying to negatively influence or change you—some intentionally, others unintentional. In those times you must ask yourself:

* Am I doing this for myself, or am I doing this because others expect me to?
* Am I happy doing what I am doing?
* Am I passionate with what I am doing?
* Am I aligned with the desires of my heart?

Discovering your passion often involves reevaluating your circle of friends. You know who the "Negative Nellies" are—those who constantly bring doubt and negativity into your life. To move forward and live your desired life, you must clear away the clutter, including negative influences. When I released the "negative Nellies" from my life, everything changed. The air felt fresher, I felt lighter, and I was happier. I could breathe more deeply, see more clearly, and fully relax. The world truly looked and felt different. I found myself waking up with joy and a renewed appreciation for life.

Now, I'm not saying you can never have a relationship with a "Negative Nelly," that is completely impossible. Unfortunately in the world we live in today you'll encounter many negative unhappy people. But what I am saying is that you'll want to keep your distance for them. Limit your time with them. See them only when necessary, love them from afar, pray for them, and celebrate with them if you must—but don't linger too long. When you notice their negativity or toxic behavior creeping in, politely excuse yourself from the room or the conversation. Be present, but don't re-accept the energy and thoughts you've worked so hard to leave behind. Let them know you're still around, but don't let them derail you from your path. Focus on the work you were called to do. Stay aligned with your GPS (God's Pathway System).

I'll never forget an experience I had years ago. I was invited to a gathering by a group of women I met through a mutual friend—we'll call her Ruby. Before attending, I asked the ladies in the group if Ruby would also be there (remember, Ruby introduced me to these women). I was shocked by their response. What they said about Ruby and why they didn't invite her was so negative and toxic that there was no way they didn't see my jaw drop. I couldn't believe what I was hearing. The negativity was relentless, and the atmosphere was suffocating. I felt so uncomfortable that I could barely move. Summoning the strength to excuse myself, I had to tell those ladies a piece of my mind before leaving. I ran out of there like I was escaping a fire.

The ugliness and toxicity in that group that night was overwhelming. Needless to say, Ruby and I never attended another event hosted by those women. They spent so much time gossiping about each other that their gatherings became pointless. Looking back, it's no surprise that the group eventually dissolved; everyone went their own way, and a few reached out to me to apologize and request that they participate in the women-empowering events I facilitated.

This experience taught me a powerful lesson: negative and toxic people will drain your energy, derail your focus, and prevent you from living the life you were intended to live. You shouldn't cut them off completely, but you must establish boundaries. Protect your peace, stay focused on your purpose, and continuously stay in alignment with your authentic self.

What I've discovered is that when you draw closer to God and His Word, people notice the change in you. They see that you're different—the way you carry yourself, how you think, and how you respond. Your focus shifts, your energy changes, and even your tolerance for nonsense decreases. It becomes clear to those around you without you needing to say a word. They begin to approach you differently, often avoiding negativity altogether because they know you won't entertain it. They recognize that you've set boundaries, and there's only so much you'll allow into your space.

When you're on the journey of self-discovery, you may find aspects of yourself that you don't particularly like. That's a good thing—it indicates that you're growing and evolving into the "new you." There's absolutely nothing wrong with recognizing areas of your life or personality that require change. In fact, it presents the perfect opportunity to begin transforming.

Often, the aspects you dislike about yourself may stem from influences of others—ideas, habits, or behaviors you adopted to fulfill someone else's expectations. This is your opportunity to shed those traits and replace them with qualities that align with who you genuinely want to be. Identify what no longer serves you and make a change.

How do you make a change? Focus on what brings you joy, peace, and fulfillment, and engage more in those activities. Let go of what no longer serves you, and replace it with habits and pursuits that align with who you're becoming. For example:

* Don't wear things you don't like; wear what makes you feel confident.
* Avoid saying things you don't believe. Express words that resonate with your truth.

* Avoid activities that deplete you. Focus on what brings you happiness, purpose and passion.

It's about finding your passion and aligning your life with what makes you feel truly alive.

One of the things I needed to change about myself was how I responded during conversations. I realized that I often reacted emotionally, blurting out responses based on my feelings at the moment instead of taking the time to consider the question or topic thoughtfully. When someone asked me a question, I would immediately jump to an emotional reaction, often without fully listening to what they were saying or allowing them to finish their thought.

This lack of reflection wasn't intentional; I had fallen into the pattern of responding emotionally. Over time, I realized this wasn't serving anyone any good. I wasn't giving myself the space to process, analyze, or even consider the broader perspective. Let's face it—politics and religion often evoke strong emotions, which is probably why people advise avoiding them in casual conversations.

Once I recognized this patterns, I consciously tried to pause, reflect, and respond more intentionally. I discovered that responding thoughtfully is not only more effective but also allows me to align my words with my values and beliefs. This change was a small yet significant step toward becoming the person I aspire to be.

Now, I take the time to genuinely listen to people—their words, the topics, and the flow of the conversation. I've learned not to respond too quickly or emotionally. Instead, I listen and wait. I reflect on my response, considering how God would want me to reply, and only after the person has finished speaking do I share my thoughts. God gave us two ears and one mouth for a reason: we are meant to listen more and speak less (LOL). It's all about shifting our mindset. It involves recognizing what you dislike about yourself and choosing to change it. Now, when I participate in conversations, I reflect on the topic, and strive to respond thoughtfully and logically, keeping my focus on the discussion.

Discovering what you dislike about yourself is a sign of growth. As you strive to become the best version of yourself, uncovering your true identity and aligning with your purpose and plan for your life, you will inevitably reveal areas that need improvement, and that's my friend is amazing! Recognizing these areas is essential and your first step. Embrace them with grace and then making the necessary changes is the second step. Growth isn't about perfection—it's about progress and the willingness to refine yourself to reflect your purpose in life.

As you discover the "new you" and transform into the person you wish to be, there will be times when small voices invade your mind. These voices will try to make you doubt yourself, dislike yourself, not believe in yourself, and even question your worth. The voices in your head will attempt to persuade you that others are talking about you, that no one cares about you, and perhaps that what you have to share adds no value to others, or no value at all.

Even when you start to truly believe in who you are and build confidence in yourself, those negative voices might still arise occasionally. But here's the good news: you can push back. Here's how:

1. **STAND FIRM IN WHO YOU ARE BECOMING.**
   You must genuinely believe in the person you are becoming. Trust in your transformation and hold on to the understanding that you are uncovering the real, authentic you. Stand firm in your self-belief and do not let doubt creep in.

2. **SPEND TIME WITH GOD.**
   Arm yourself with God's Word by memorizing Bible verses that provide strength and encouragement. Listen to praise and worship music to fill your space with positivity and dispel negative voices. Create moments for spiritual meditation to balance your mind and spirit, keeping you grounded in truth.

When you focus on God's presence, the "demon talk" loses its power.

3. **MASTER YOUR MINDSET.**

 As Bob Proctor famously states, "What you think about is what you will bring about." You have control over what you allow into your mind. Program your thoughts with positive affirmations to counter negativity as it tries to creep in. The moment those negative voices begin to speak, stop them immediately and take control of your thoughts. A great method to use is the 5 Second Rule by Mel Robbins. It's a simple but powerful tool for mastering your mindset and taking action. It works by counting "5-4-3-2-1" and then physically moving or making a decision before your brain has a chance to talk you out of it. This rule interrupts fear, doubt, and hesitation, helping you build confidence and take control of your thoughts and behaviors in just five seconds.

Remember, you are stronger than the negativity that tries to derail you. By believing in yourself, spending time with God, and mastering your mindset, you can overcome anything. Stay focused on your journey, and trust that God is with you every step of the way.

When you discover who you are and how you want to live, you gain the power to create the environment you desire and control what and who enters your space. Understanding your identity, your beliefs, God's plan for your life, and your purpose equips you to build an atmosphere that wards off negativity and "demon talks." This clarity allows you to surround yourself with supportive people, brings you peace and uplifting influences that keep you focused on your path. Everyone needs to be around the right people. I often say, "As long as I'm alive, you are never alone." God never intended for us to live in isolation. Genesis 2:18 says, "The LORD God said, "It is not good for the man to be alone. I will make a helper suitable for him."

This is why it's important to find individuals who will walk with you through life—people who are positive, uplifting, and focused on empowering and inspiring others. Surround yourself with those who are honest, respectful, and genuine with you because they truly love you and want the best for you.

Clarity comes from action, not just thought. It often shows up when you begin moving forward, even if you're unsure—because each step teaches you something new about yourself, your purpose, and what truly matters. Clarity also grows through quiet moments with God, reflection, and being honest about what aligns with your values, passions, and calling. The Bible serves as your ultimate GPS, guiding you toward your destiny, clearing your mind, and helping you stay focused on your purpose. However, clarity can also be derived from various other resources, such as meditation, church, podcasts (like my "Sip with Sidrid" episodes), life transformational coaches (like me—LOL), articles, YouTube videos, praise and worship music, just to name a few resources.

Let me emphasize the value of having a coach in your life. A great coach can help you set and achieve your goals, build confidence, and deepen your self-belief—and even guide you closer to Jesus Christ, if that's your wish. As a coach, I genuinely enjoy working with clients eager to grow, transform, and enhance their lives. Witnessing their transformations and breakthroughs is truly invaluable.

Confidence is rooted in understanding who you are and recognizing the "key ingredients" that make you unique. Too often, we look outward and blame the world for our circumstances, but the truth is that everything begins within us. We transform the world around us by first transforming ourselves.

The world will not impact you—unless you let it. We've been taught to believe that our lives are controlled by outside influences, like the media. However, the media actually reflects our actions. Our behaviors, beliefs, and identity shape the world around us. When you take ownership of your life and align your life with who you were meant to be, you'll find the confidence and clarity to live fully and intentionally.

CHAPTER 8

Do Differently To Become Different

*"Move Different If You Want Different -
Old Keys Will Never Open New Doors"*

~ Leo Tolstoy ~

To initiate something new today, you must first consider becoming different. It's no longer about the "old you" but embracing the "new you." This process begins with reflecting on the patterns and/or behaviors that need to change and deciding to change them; to take action. Sometimes, change is a choice we make intentionally; other times, life circumstances push us into it. Either way, doing things differently starts with the choice of wanting to become different.

Think of it like driving a car: you can't press the brakes and the accelerator at the same time. If you try, the car will break down. Similarly, in life, you must choose a direction and commit to it. To change, you must evaluate your life and determine what needs to shift. Some changes are straightforward. For instance, if you want to lose weight, you might decide to walk for 10 or 15 minutes each day. That simple action can lead to significant results over time. The key is taking action; doing something different generates the outcomes you desire.

Let me share a personal experience that highlights the importance of change. While writing this book, I encountered a health challenge that turned my world upside down. For about a month, I dealt with an overwhelming thirst that never seemed to dissipate. No matter how much water I drank, I remained thirsty. I consumed so much that I started to feel as though I might be harming my body. At the same time, I was frequently visiting the bathroom.

One day, my husband gently pointed out, "I think you're showing symptoms of diabetes." His words struck me hard. I remember looking at him in disbelief and responding, "Please don't say that where the universe can hear. I rebuke it in the name of Jesus." I was upset that he even implied it, though I knew he meant no harm.

To my surprise, he was right. A week later, I could no longer ignore my symptoms. The persistent thirst, my raspy voice, and the painful dryness in my throat each morning prompted me to see a doctor. After conducting some tests, the doctor referred me straight to the ER. My blood sugar exceeded 400, and my A1C was 10.1. That night, I received a diagnosis of Type 2 Diabetes.

For anyone who has faced a similar diagnosis, you'll understand how life-changing it can be. At 50 years old, I suddenly found myself starting over. I had to learn what to eat, when to eat, and how to manage my medications. I set alarms to remind myself to take insulin before bed. I had to determine which foods were best for me and which ones I needed to avoid. The days of eating or drinking whatever I wanted without a second thought were gone.

I had to think differently, which meant I had to act differently. Every bite I took required consideration—how many carbs were in it? How much sugar? I learned to balance my meals, ensure I ate three times a day, avoid skipping meals, and include healthy snacks when necessary. My insulin doses varied based on what I ate that day, so I had to stay vigilant and mindful.

This experience taught me that meaningful change isn't just about deciding to act differently—it's about committing to becoming a new person. Change requires effort, consistency, and above all, a willingness to adapt to a new way of life.

Does this sound exhausting to you yet? Let me tell you—it was. For crying out loud, it was overwhelming in every sense of the word. And that doesn't even account for the endless doctor visits I had to make to learn everything I needed about managing diabetes. Did you know that after being diagnosed diabetic, you're referred to an entire team of specialists?

* A Primary Care Physician (PCP) to helps you manage your overall health, and coordinates your care with specialists.
* An Endocrinologist oversees your diabetes and insulin levels.
* A Pulmonologist examines your lungs to confirm that there's no underlying damage.
* A Pharmacist to instruct you on the proper way to administer insulin and manage medications.
* A Nutritionist who offers you advice and guidance on what to eat, and more importantly, on what to avoid.
* An Ophthalmologist or an Optometrist to make sure your vision hasn't been impacted.
* A Podiatrist examines your feet for changes in color, dryness, or sores that may lead to complications.
* A Nephrologist to make sure there are no kidney issues and that they are functioning properly.

The sheer number of appointments, information, and changes felt like an avalanche. I really had to think and act differently! I had no choice but to adapt quickly. For me, choosing to live differently wasn't optional—it was essential. If I wanted to survive, I had to embrace the new reality of my life and commit to taking the necessary steps to get healthier.

Now, maybe your situation isn't as critical as mine, or perhaps it's more so, but the importance of doing things differently remains vital. For you, it might be as simple as walking for 10 minutes a day or eliminating toxicity from your life. It could involve deciding to go to college, starting a new job or career, or improving your diet; or maybe it's getting chemo 5 times a week or getting infusion or dialysis every week. Alternatively, it might mean taking the time to reconnect with God after too long spent being distant. Whatever it may be, embracing change requires intention and action. You must make the necessary adjustments to become your authentic self—the person you are meant to be. It's not always easy, but it's always worthwhile.

But how do you start doing things differently? What steps should you take to change truly? First, you need to make the choice. You must decide you're ready to change and commit to taking the necessary steps to do things differently. This begins with believing that **YOU MATTER**—that your choices and growth are significant. Others may disagree with your decisions, but their opinions should not sway you from focusing on your goals. Listening to the views of others won't bring you closer to realizing your dreams or becoming the person you were meant to be. Their opinions don't determine your value.

What matters is that you become the person you aspire to be, achieve the goals you want to reach, and fulfill the purpose you know in your heart you were has created for. This often involves stepping outside your comfort zone and adapting to unforeseen circumstances. For example:

* You may envision advancing in your career, but your desired position requires relocating to another state.
* Maybe you've always imagined having biological children, but you've been told it isn't possible.
* Perhaps you've intended to attend college, but you choose to remain at home to care for a sick parent.
* Or you might find yourself prepared to marry someone you believed was Mr. Right, only to uncover just before the wedding that he was "Mr. Right Now."

Life is full of curveballs that can make us doubt ourselves or force us to pivot. But that doesn't mean we should give up. It simply means we must reassess the situation and adjust our course without abandoning our goals. Think of life as a GPS: when there's a detour, the GPS recalculates your route, but the destination remains the same.

We may sometimes go through unexpected valleys we didn't want to face. However, in those moments, it's vital to remember that God is faithful. If you trust Him, He will guide you, protect you, and provide a way out during life's toughest challenges. Frequently, the things we least want to do are precisely those that shape us into who we are meant to become.

For me, becoming a Type 2 diabetic wasn't part of my life plan, and it wasn't due to a love of sweets. It occurred because I wasn't eating properly. I often skipped meals, sometimes going 12 to 15 hours without eating—surviving on just a cup of coffee. I maintained this for over five years, which ultimately led to my body breaking down and developing Type 2 diabetes. According to an article from UCSF Diabetes Education Online, "The liver makes sugar when you need it… When you're not eating—especially overnight or between meals—the body must make its own sugar. The liver supplies sugar or glucose by converting glycogen into glucose in a process called glycogenolysis."

My poor eating patterns forced my body into survival mode, ultimately leading to my diagnosis and a critical decision: I had to start doing things differently to live differently. I'm proud to share that, by making the right choice making and taking the necessary actions, I was able to reverse my Type 2 Diabetes in only eight months. My diagnosis revealed to me what I was doing to my body and I took the opportunity to turn things around. To reverse diabetes, I had to choose to do things differently.

I had to learn how to care for myself, and I put everything I learned from all the physicians I consulted into action. As excited as I was to reverse diabetes, because I was 200% sure that I did not want to be another statistic, many people doubted me—family members, friends, and even doctors. Some rolled their eyes at me when I told them. Some didn't believe I could reverse diabetes because they had never seen it done. Others thought it was too difficult, and some simply dismissed my intentions, thinking I wouldn't follow through like so many others.

But here I am, living proof that doing things differently can produce extraordinary results. *Doing things differently involves making changes that transform your life and help you become the best version of yourself.* Sure, it's not always easy—it can feel limiting at times, like having to monitor my sugar intake—but I did it because it made me healthier. By becoming healthier, I can step into the person I'm meant to be, accomplish my goals, and fulfill the assignments God created me for.

I also had to confront and eliminate my internal toxicity and the negative people, patterns, and habits that were holding me back. It wasn't easy, but it was necessary—because doing the inner work is what allowed me to stand here today and help you chase your dreams and step into the best version of yourself. We all carry things—whether it's toxic thoughts, draining relationships, or unhealthy habits—that we must let go of in order to fully embrace who we were always meant to be. For me, doing things differently meant creating balance in every aspect of my life—physically, emotionally, socially, spiritually, and mentally. This balance has become my new lifestyle and has been key to my transformation.

For you, my fabulous readers, doing differently involves identifying the aspects of your life that no longer align with who you aspire to be and substituting them with habits, patterns, people, and choices that support your goals and dreams. Examine your life. Identifying your needs, goals, and values is the first step toward creating the lifestyle you desire.

There are only few guarantees in life that we cannot change or escape: death and taxes. However, there is one guarantee we can influence—*change your mindset, and you will change your life.* When you choose to shift your mindset toward living your best life and take the necessary actions, you will indeed live your best life. The key is to stay focused on what you truly want. Don't let distractions or doubts derail you from your goals. Remain committed to your plan—to your internal GPS—and allow God to guide your journey. With His guidance, you'll enjoy a happier, more fulfilling life. Another guarantee in life is the ability to make choices. We can determine most of the who, what, where, when, why, and how of our lives. Becoming a better version of yourself starts with a choice: the choice to commit. You must decide what you want to change in your life to create the future you desire. To improve your life, you need to prioritize yourself.

I didn't fully understand what being healthy meant until I was forced to change my habits after being diagnosed with Type 2 diabetes. The moment I received the diagnosis, I knew I had to shift my mindset to prioritize my health. Suddenly, it wasn't about eating whatever I wanted, whenever I wanted. It wasn't about skipping meals just because I wasn't hungry. It wasn't about avoiding exercise because I didn't enjoy it or thought I was too busy. I had to commit to learning how to be healthier. That meant educating myself about diabetes—reading books, watching videos, and meeting with professionals like a nutritionist and a pharmacist. I learned how to give myself insulin and understand how my blood sugar levels were affected by what I ate, drank, and whether exercised or didn't. It felt like starting from scratch, learning to live all over again, but this time, with my health as the priority.

Was it exhausting? Absolutely. But if I wanted to live a better life, I needed to improve. I had to change my mindset and focus on my well-being like never before, even when it felt uncomfortable. I had to embrace discomfort to become healthier. This journey taught me a profound truth: *"What you think might be working against you could actually working for you."* I could have seen my diabetes diagnosis as purely negative, but when I chose to find the silver lining, I realized it was a turning point. Honestly, I'm probably healthier now than I've been in the last ten years. I now eat balanced meals, have at least three meals daily, drink less of what I don't need, stay hydrated with plenty of water, and walk more then I ever had. Although it wasn't easy to make these changes, they were essential for my growth, health, and happiness. If there's one takeaway from my experience, it's this: *change begins with a choice.* By shifting your mindset and committing to doing better for yourself, you can transform your life in ways you never thought possible.

Before being diagnosed with diabetes, I would easily accept any food or drink offered to me. However, after my diagnosis, I had to remind myself to consider what was being offered and how much sugar it contained. It was a complete mindset transformation, and it was very difficult at first. Nevertheless, I was willing to face discomfort to reverse my diabetes and achieve the life I wanted. Was it easy? Of course not; it was all about transforming my mind. For fifty years, I could eat and drink whatever I wanted without a second thought. Now, thinking about what I consume and how my body would react has been a tough adjustment. But you find a way to make it work. I understood the consequences of not choosing a healthier lifestyle. For me, the thought of becoming blind, having a leg amputated, losing an organ, being on dialysis, or developing other health issues due to my habits was absolutely unacceptable. So, I committed to changing my lifestyle to live longer and happier. Becoming healthier, changing my habits, doing things differently, and striving to be the best version of myself have ensured that I could become a new me—a better, healthier person. I wanted (and still want to) live my best life, so I made it happen.

To live the life you want, you'll need to do what others won't do. You must embrace the unexpected and the uncomfortable. Most people are unwilling to work hard and take the necessary steps to achieve their goals, fulfill their desires, or become the person they've always wanted to be. You, on the other hand, are ready; you are different. You have what it takes to make it happen, to prioritize yourself, and to tackle the discomfort because you are prepared to become the person you've been striving to be.

If you've been wondering what you need to change to become the best version of yourself, start by taking an honest look at your life. Write down the things that you're unhappy with—the areas that feel unfulfilling or out of alignment. Consider the following:

* The aspects you know you want to change.
* Things that add no value to your life.
* The habits or actions you engage in, even if you don't genuinely believe in them.
* The factors that lead to sadness, stress, or depression.
* The situations or individuals that frustrate you or trigger negative emotions.

Your list can include personal behaviors or relationships that need re-evaluation. Perhaps you've realized that you're a people pleaser—constantly striving to satisfy your boss, your kids, best friend, parent, spouse, or even those so-called "friends" who don't genuinely support you. Maybe you've neglected to take time for yourself, always putting others first and now feeling drained and unseen. Or perhaps you're overworked, logging 50 to 60 hours a week, and missing out on life's precious moments—your kids' activities, family gatherings, girls' nights out, or holiday celebrations. Maybe your hard work is for an ungrateful boss who neither respects nor values you.

Maybe it's time to change how you see yourself when you look in the mirror—to recognize the value, beauty, and brilliance of who you are. You are a spectacular masterpiece created by God. It's time to embrace that truth. Maybe you need to change the way you speak about yourself—to others and to yourself. Do you undervalue or underestimate your worth? Do you let fear hold you back? Perhaps it's time to replace fear with confidence and boldly step into the unknown. After all, if God's got your back, what is there to be afraid of?

This is your moment to start creating the life you desire, the life that aligns with the path God has laid out for you. Let's identify what needs to change, commit to those changes, and take action! It's time to embrace your purpose and create the life you were always meant to lead. The journey starts now, and it begins with you—let's make it happen!

Examine closely the aspects of your life that make you uncomfortable—those behaviors, habits, or choices that don't align with your authentic self. These are the areas that require your attention and commitment to change. Your list may be long or short; the length is irrelevant. What truly matters is that each item on that list signifies something preventing you from being your true self.

When you choose to change your inner self, you are choosing to reveal and embrace your true self. God has given us the remarkable gift of free will, which allows us to make decisions that shape our lives. With His guidance and Spirit, we can create a life full of purpose, experience His blessings, and become the person He meant for us to be.

As you start making these changes and aligning your life with your God-given purpose, something amazing happens: your confidence grows. You'll start to truly love and appreciate yourself as you recognize the masterpiece God has created within you. You'll understand your immense value—not just to God, but to your family, your true friends, and to this world. You are worthy, you are valuable, and you are deeply loved. Embrace this journey of change and step into the life you were always meant to live.

On the next page, begin today writing down your list. Start with the things you are ready to change—those areas of your life that no longer serve you or align with your purpose.

I am changing...

Now that you have created your list, it's important to realize that transformation begins with a choice—a choice to change—and it starts with a change of heart. True transformation occurs when we are honest with ourselves about what we genuinely desire. When that change is authentic, your true self begins to shine. The beauty of these changes is that, as you embrace them, they feel natural and effortless because they guide you toward the YOU you've always longed to be.

With true change, joy fills your heart, making life more meaningful. You begin to appreciate the world around you, value the things that bring you happiness, and surround yourself with the right people—those who uplift and inspire you. Negative voices and toxic influences have no place in your life anymore. Each day, you gain a deeper understanding of the importance of living according to your own beliefs and values. When you recognize your worth—to God, to yourself, and to the world—you embrace the fullness of your authentic self. In this realization, you discover purpose, peace, and the freedom to live as the person you were always meant to be.

Making changes and doing things differently are crucial because they shape the person you want to become. Choice and change are processes that cannot be avoided. As Albert Einstein wisely said, "Doing the same thing repeatedly and expecting different results is the definition of insanity." If you want a better life and to become a better person, change is not just necessary—it's transformative. To grow into the person you aspire to be, you must address what isn't working in your life and intentionally focus on doing things differently. Change begins with a decision; although it's optional, it is essential for progress.

When I was in junior high school, there was a girl and her group of friends—let's call them the "mean female bullies" (MFBs)—who terrorized many girls at school. For some reason, the ringleader targeted me. Every morning and afternoon, she would wait at the bottom of the stairs, trying to trip me as I went up or down. If she failed, she'd find other ways to torment me—walking behind me to pull my hair or throwing things across the room to hit me in the head.

At the time, I didn't realize it, but her bullying taught me an important lesson: how to empower myself and refuse to be a victim. Her actions pushed me to decide that I wanted something different for myself—and for others. I refused to give her the power to intimidate me or define my worth. Victimization is a choice, and after enduring several weeks of her harassment, I chose to think differently, act differently, and take action.

One day, after one of her attempts to trip me, I reacted. I grabbed her foot, made her fall, and stood my ground. She seemed ready for a fight, so I gave her one and I fought back and won. While I'm not necessarily proud of the physical confrontation (or maybe I am?), and I don't promote violence, I realized then that I had reclaimed my power.

That experience taught me to stand up for myself, refuse to be intimidated, and never allow anyone to treat me with disrespect or cruelty. For her behavior toward me to change, I had to alter how I responded. I needed to think differently, act differently, and do differently. Through this experience, I learned that I matter. I shouldn't accept mistreatment simply because someone doesn't like me or feels insecure about themselves. Empowering yourself starts with recognizing your worth and refusing to let anyone diminish it. By choosing to change how I handled the situation, I not only stopped her bullying—I also learned that I have the strength to define how others treat me and to stand up for the life I deserve. I realized I had to approach things differently—not only for myself but also for others who might feel powerless. I needed to act and respond in a way that would compel the bully and the mean-girl clique to treat me—and others—better.

To become better people, we must first identify what needs to change within ourselves and then commit to making those changes. I wanted to be a student who wasn't afraid of anything or anyone. I tried to encourage others to come to school without feeling like they had to walk on eggshells around those bullies. I wanted to inspire my peers to stand up for what they believed in and reject the things they no longer wanted to endure. To do that, I had to defend my beliefs and values. I needed to make it clear to those bullies that I wasn't going to tolerate being mistreated, devalued, or disrespected. By standing up for myself, I not only empowered myself, I also empowered others to do the same.

Here's what I found to be truly amazing: when you start becoming the person you're meant to be, you naturally attract people who share your values and energy. By standing up for what I believed in, I gained the confidence to stop the MFBs in their tracks. As I did, I noticed a ripple effect—other students began believing in themselves and finding the courage to confront their own bullies.

One of my favorite quotes by Dennis and Wendy Mannering perfectly sums this up:

"Attitudes are contagious; is yours worth catching?"
Take a moment to reflect on that. Is your attitude—your beliefs, your values—something others would want to emulate? Are you inspiring those around you to embrace their authentic selves?

I genuinely believe that when you choose to make a difference in your own life, you naturally inspire others to change theirs. By embodying authenticity, courage, and self-respect, you empower others to do the same. When you live as your true self, you create a space for those around you to also be authentically real.

Side Note: If you are being bullied or abused in any way, I encourage you to speak up. Reach out to someone you trust, report it, or tell someone who can help. Make your voice heard— you deserve better. Staying silent can feel more effortless in the moment, but it often allows the bully to continue their behavior unchecked. Silence can unintentionally send the message that what they are doing is acceptable. You can take a stand and stop the bullying—not just for yourself, but for others, too. Change starts with you, and by choosing to speak out, you can catalyze that change.

If you're facing bullying or abuse, please know that help is available. Don't hesitate to reach out to a Crisis Counselor Center near you. You can also text HOME to 741741 to connect with a trained Crisis Counselor, who is available to support you 24/7. You are not alone; there are people who care and want to help.

CHAPTER 9

Create Your Plan

"If you fail to plan, you plan to fail."

~ Benjamin Franklin ~

Paul J. Meyer, founder of the Success Motivation Institute, introduced the "Wheel of Life" in the 1960's as a tool for individuals to set goals, identify their needs, and achieve balance in their lives. I like to call it "The Wheel of Possibilities" because of the endless opportunities it offers for growth and transformation.

In this book, I've included my step-by-step version of the "Wheel of Possibilities" process. This guide will help you identify the best areas to focus on first as you begin creating the life you desire. This personal development tool evaluates and balances eight key areas of your life, providing a clear picture of your current happiness levels. It will also help you determine where you might want to start making changes to align your life with your goals and dreams. Let's work through this exercise together. For you to truly benefit, it's essential that you're 100% honest with yourself as you evaluate all eight key areas. Below is an example of what a "Wheel of Possibility" should look like.

Take a moment to create your own Wheel of Possibilities using the blank template below. For each key area, mark a dot on the scale from 1 to 10 to represent your current level of happiness—1 being very dissatisfied and unhappy, and 10 being very satisfied and happy (refer to the sample Wheel of Possibilities below). After rating yourself in each area, shade in the sections of the wheel starting from the center (number 1) and moving outward to reflect your rating level. For instance, if you rate your health and wellness a 6, you will shade up to the sixth section, filling in towards the center of the wheel without exceeding your dotted line. Repeat this for each area until your wheel is complete. Use the Wheel of Possibilities on the next page for this exercise.

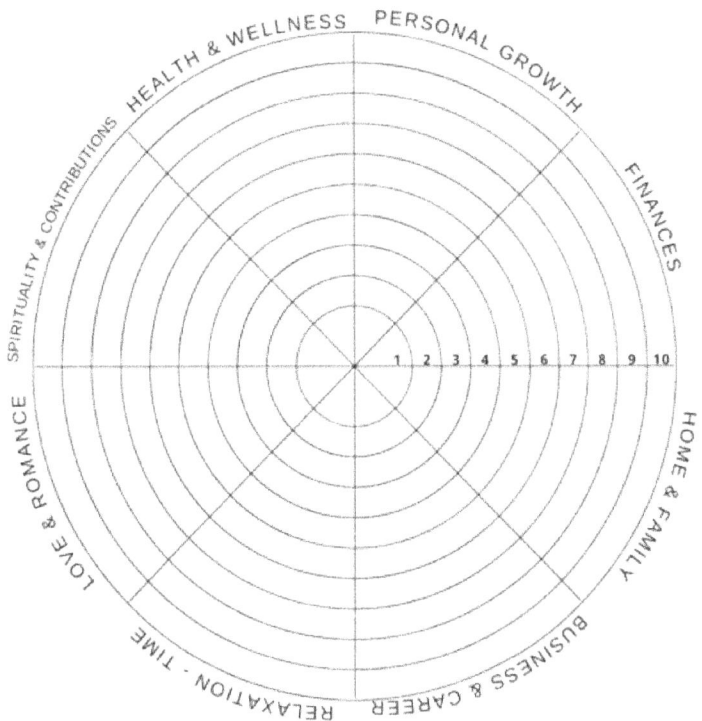
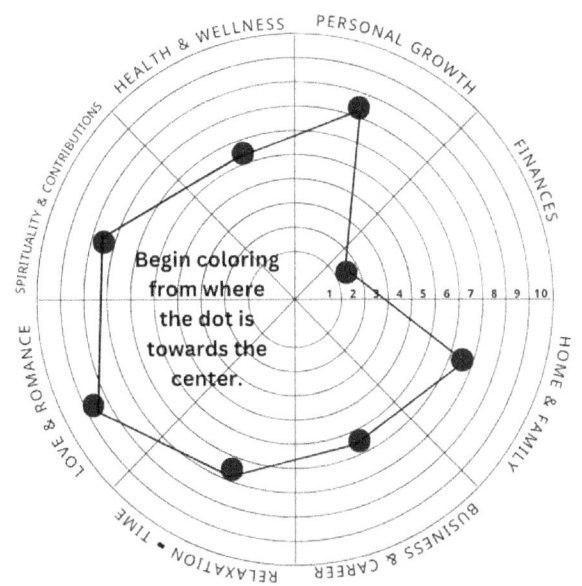

Creating the right plan begins with establishing goals that align with your aspirations. To become the best version of yourself, you must first determine what it will take to get there. Reflect on the changes or additions you currently desire in your life, and then set small, actionable objectives that will help you move toward your goal — **devising the plan.**

Personal growth is closely linked to goal setting, as goals offer direction, motivation, and a sense of purpose. They help us fulfill our desires and encourage us to achieve more. You'll know you've developed the right plan when your goals steer you toward enhancing your personal growth. These goals might encompass being more open-minded, practicing gratitude, discovering your passion or purpose, making informed decisions, learning new skills, living by your values, adopting healthy habits, nurturing a positive circle of friends, finding the right partner, eliminating toxicity from your life, or realizing any other aspirations. The world is your oyster—what you accomplish is entirely up to you.

Let's Work on a Goal Together:

To get started, review your Wheel of Possibilities from the previous pages. Select one key area (category, for example Personal Growth or Finances) to focus on for this exercise. Just choose one for now. Next, go to the next page and write down the category/goal in step #1.

To assist you in writing your goal you'll want to utilize the **SMART** acronym:

1. **S**pecific: Clearly articulate your goal. The more specific you are, the more precise the path to success will be.
2. **M**easurable: Break your goal into daily tasks. Tracking your progress allows you to see how far you've come, helping you remain motivated and focused.
3. **A**chievable: Ensure your goal is realistic and attainable based on your current situation.
4. **R**elevant: Align your goals with your identity and values. They should be meaningful, purposeful, and in harmony with your true self. Consistency in pursuing relevant goals leads to success.
5. **T**ime-Bound: Set a deadline for achieving your goal. Specify a particular date and year to ensure accountability.

This process was designed to help you set effective personal and professional goals. This guide will empower you to discover your values and clarify your aspirations. Edwin A. Locke was a prominent psychologist known for his extensive research on goal-setting theory, and he famously stated, "At the heart of effective goal setting lies a deep understanding of oneself." In other words, to have meaningful and achievable goals, we must first have a clear and honest understanding of who we are. This includes:

1. Your values and beliefs: Understanding what truly matters to you ensures that your goals align with your core values and stay authentic.
2. Your Strengths and Weaknesses: Understanding your abilities enables you to establish realistic and achievable goals while recognizing areas for improvement.
3. Your Desires and Passions: Understanding what motivates and excites you ensures that your goals are meaningful and satisfying.
4. Your Current Circumstances: Acknowledging your current situation, limitations, and resources helps you formulate a plan tailored to your reality.

In essence, understanding yourself—your needs, motivations, and purpose—enables you to set goals that are meaningful, relevant, and aligned with your true self, thus increasing the likelihood of achieving them.

Let's begin…

GOAL SETTING:

1. What is the goal I want to work on?

_____
_____
_____
_____

2. Why do I want to achieve this goal?

_____
_____
_____
_____

3. Which obstacles could I be confronted with?

_____
_____
_____
_____

4. How will I achieve my goal? What do I need to do to achieve my goal?

_____
_____
_____
_____

5. Why is my goal important to me?

_____
_____
_____
_____

6. What is the deadline for my goal?

_____
_____
_____
_____

When I decided to launch Sidrid Rivera Enterprises (SRE) and step into my role as a Business and Life Transformational Mindset Coach, I started with prayer and a clear, strategic business plan. I outlined my reasons for creating this business, the goals I aimed to achieve, and the steps needed to build its infrastructure. I envisioned what SRE would look like, the impact we would have, and how we would serve others.

The word 'manifest' means "to make evident or certain by showing or displaying what you desire." For me, that desire was to create an empowering, inspiring, and successful transformational mindset coaching company. I had a vision, prayed for what my heart desired, and set clear goals to turn that vision into reality. Did I "fake it till I made it"? No. Instead, I leaned on faith—I chose to **"Faith It Till You Make It."**

What do I mean by "faith"? I mean trusting that the nudge I felt in my gut and the excitement about my vision were divinely inspired and destined to happen. I created a SMART goal—Specific, Measurable, Attainable, Relevant, and Time-bound—that outlined exactly what I wanted to achieve. I ensured my plan was well-structured and launched at just the right moment. This clarity and alignment was so impactful that we had clients ready for coaching even before officially launching the business.

When you pursue your vision, heed that inner nudge, and align yourself with God's purpose, aspirations transform plans into reality, converting dreams into businesses and elevating broken financial situations to a state of abundance. Determining whether you've made the right plan comes from the outcomes you observe. It's about experiencing true happiness, feeling passionate, and enjoying life without worrying about what others think or say. It's about trusting your path, discarding unhelpful "ingredients" or suggestions from others, and allowing your inner GPS to guide you. Developing the right plan helps you wake up in peace, worry-free, and appreciate the air you breathe. It's about finding joy in life, recognizing your true friends, and living in harmony with God's purpose for you. When your plan aligns with God's path, you feel fulfilled—you know you're exactly where you're meant to be.

Your plan is yours and yours alone. It's not about comparing your journey to someone else's or letting others dictate your choices. Each person's plan is unique and tailored to their purpose. That purpose is driven by your passion(s), and you have the privilege to shape it into what you desire. Becoming the person you were intended to be is the ultimate achievement—a sense of completion. There's no imitation, no pretending, and no exhaustion from trying to be someone you're not. There's simply the authentic, fulfilled, and fully real YOU.

Don't get too caught up in ensuring your plan is perfect. If the plan doesn't work, change the plan—but never change the goal. Your goal reflects your desire, purpose, and passion. Plans can and will change. Life is unpredictable, and sometimes circumstances force us to adjust. That doesn't mean your plan was wrong; it simply means it needs a little tweaking.

Imagine it as if you are buying your first Louis Vuitton purse—one of the most iconic and luxurious accessories in the fashion world. Perhaps you've saved and planned every detail to buy your dream LV purse. You're excited, confident, and prepared to make the purchase. You enter the store, spot the perfect purse, and ask the sales associate to retrieve it for you. However, the associate apologizes and says, "I'm so sorry, we're sold out of that style."

Does that mean your plan to buy the purse was a mistake? Of course not. It just means you may need to adjust your approach. Perhaps you'll check another store, purchase it online, or wait for it to restock. You'll still get your dream purse, just not in the exact way you initially envisioned. Don't let frustration over a change of plans distract you. Your goal remains the same, even if the path to achieving it changes. In life, our plans might need to be adjusted, reworked, or completely rerouted at times. But remember, you are still in control of what you create, what you decide, and who you become. Sometimes, those unexpected detours can lead to an even better outcome.

As Jamie Kern Lima wisely states, "Rejection is God's Protection." Perhaps not getting that purse at that moment was God protecting you, maybe from losing it, having it stolen, or spending money you might need for an unforeseen circumstance. Regardless of the reason, be open to change. Sometimes, the unexpected is precisely what we need. Re-evaluate your plan, make the necessary adjustments, and restart with confidence. Always ensure your changes align with your goals, purpose, vision, desires, and relationship with God. Remember, the destination remains the same even if the route changes. Trust the process and keep moving forward.

CHAPTER 10

Expect Differently

*"You were never meant to stay the same.
Dare to be different."*

~ Sidrid Rivera ~

In 2007, my husband Ricky wasn't feeling well. He had flu-like symptoms—fever, vomiting, weakness, and loss of appetite. For two days, he stayed home to rest, but he wasn't getting better. One morning, he came downstairs and asked me to make him toast. I prepared a slice of bread and some soup for him. He ate as much as he could and then decided to return to bed.

As Ricky was going up the stairs, I suddenly heard a loud thumping noise. Alarmed, I rushed to the stairs and found him lying there—he had fallen and was unable to make it to the top. He was so weak that he couldn't lift himself. Thankfully, my brother-in-law was at home and helped carry Ricky upstairs. I immediately called 911.

I quickly got Ricky dressed just as the ambulance arrived. What happened next left me in shock. At the hospital, the doctor informed me that Ricky could have died that day if we hadn't brought him in when we did. I was confused—how could the flu be so dangerous? I still believed that this was what we were dealing with.

Later that day, after the doctors conducted numerous exams, I discovered the truth. Ricky had been fighting with our new health insurance company because we had recently switched health plans, but the insurance company had not received the necessary documentation from his physician to approve his medication. What Ricky didn't tell me was that he had run out of insulin and had not taken any insulin for three days.

If you know anything about diabetes, as a type 1 diabetic, you know insulin is a lifesaving necessity. Without it, the body cannot regulate blood sugar levels, which can lead to severe complications. Since Ricky hadn't taken his insulin for three days, his organs were beginning to shut down. This explained why he couldn't keep food down, struggled to breathe, had a fever, and was gravely ill.

This experience was a wake-up call for Ricky. To expect different results, he had to do things differently. He needed to decide to take better control of his health and ensure he would never let his body reach such a critical state again.

Ricky implemented several significant changes:

*   He started communicating more effectively with his doctors, insurance provider, and me, his wife, to ensure he always had timely access to insulin.
*   He taught himself about his condition and the significance of managing it effectively.
*   He consulted a nutritionist to discover how to make healthier food choices that supported his treatment plan.
*   He collaborated closely with a pharmacist to comprehend the medications he was using and their functioning.

Ricky approached things differently to achieve the desired results needed for survival and success. He became his own advocate, taking control of his health and making proactive changes. As a result, he was able to enjoy a healthier, more fulfilling life free from unnecessary worries. He ensured the timely delivery of his insulin by effectively communicating with his health insurance provider. In short, because Ricky chose to take action and do what was necessary, he achieved the results he desired. Through these changes, Ricky not only improved his health but also empowered himself to take proactive steps in managing his diabetes. This journey taught us the critical importance of self-advocacy, education, and consistent action in overcoming life's challenges.

Ricky asks the right questions to ensure he receives the best care possible. He shares his story openly, using his experiences to inspire and guide others in taking better care of themselves. Instead of feeling ashamed or embarrassed, Ricky embraces his journey and is passionate about helping others become the best version of themselves. Today, Ricky experiences life differently; he is happier, healthier, and has a renewed sense of purpose.

In life, you won't always receive applause, support, or even kindness. People will offer their opinions, advice, and criticism—sometimes unsolicited, often uninformed—and not all of it will be positive or even helpful. But let's be real... why should that matter? Why give someone else the power to dictate how you feel about yourself? Their opinion isn't your truth. Their perspective is limited. They haven't walked in your shoes, cried your tears, or fought your battles. You don't need validation from people who weren't assigned to your purpose. God already approved you. So instead of chasing approval, chase alignment—with who you are, whose you are, and where you're going. Because the loudest voice in your life should never be theirs—it should BE YOURS.

If there's something in your life that you don't like, you have the power to change it—because it's your life. If others can't accept who you are or the growth you've embraced, that's a reflection of them—not you. You must remain true to yourself. Those who truly love you will love you regardless of your changes. For those who criticize you, it's time to set boundaries or eliminate their negativity from your life.

As Tony Robbins famously says, **"Change your story, change your life."** You have the potential and the power to rewrite your story and create the changes you desire. Not everyone will be happy with the person you are becoming—and that's perfectly okay. The sooner you accept this truth, the faster you'll become the person you want to be. No matter the steps you're taking to become the best version of yourself, there will always be people who are unhappy or unsupportive. However, as long as you remain authentic and have peace in your heart, no one else's opinion should matter. **This is your life to live.**

To continue embracing your authentic self and building genuine connections with those around you, I believe it's essential to place God at the center of your life. For me, developing a deeper relationship with God and immersing myself in His Word has formed the foundation of my journey toward becoming the best version of myself. And here's the beautiful truth: God isn't finished with me yet—this masterpiece is still a work in progress! And He's not finished with you as well. He is still working within you so that you can become the masterpiece he created you to become.

As you strive to become the best version of yourself, it's crucial to recognize that you must *adjust your expectations* in your new life. Learning to anticipate change will help you avoid feeling blindsided. As I have mentioned earlier not everyone will support the person you are becoming or will they agree with the progress you are making. I love how Mel Robbins says it… "Let Them!" Let them feel that way, think that way, look at you that way. Let Them do them, because you need to do you! There will be individuals who are uncomfortable with your growth—whether it's becoming healthier, pursuing further education, expanding your business, strengthening your marriage, improving relationships with your children or in-laws, landing the job position you've always wanted, changing your career, or even finding Mr. or Ms. Right. Some people won't be pleased with how your life is evolving—or, should I say, how you're transforming your life. Expect that, and learn be ok with that.

When you prepare yourself for this reality, you'll be able to identify who genuinely loves and supports you and who doesn't. Knowing this can make heartache less painful and help you maintain focus on your journey. As you focus on becoming the best version of yourself, it's important not to place expectations on others. Expectations often lead to disappointment, pain, or sadness when they aren't met. Instead, let go of expecting support or validation from others. When you release expectations, every moment becomes a gift, and every act of kindness or encouragement feels like a beautiful surprise.

As you become the best version of yourself, you'll attract those who embrace your new persona. These are the people who will support you, inquire about the changes you've made, and relish spending time with you. Some may even say, "I want what she's having!" Your circle of influence will evolve, and you'll begin to draw in people who resonate with your authentic self—individuals who genuinely value the real you.

Reaching this destination—your authenticity—is a significant achievement. You've evolved from feeling stuck, unhappy, or unfulfilled to experiencing freedom and joy as the person you were always meant to be. This transformation requires effort: engaging with new people, forming meaningful connections, seeking fresh opportunities, and living the life you've always desired. It demands faith and intentionality to live in a way that others can only dream of.

Your life will change because you are no longer the same. The person you've become adds meaning and purpose to your life, and that's something incredibly powerful and worth celebrating. You've chosen to raise your standards, embrace change, and take control of your destiny—and for that, you should be genuinely proud.

The first time I truly experienced the difference between being authentic and not being genuine with myself and others, I felt an overwhelming sense of peace—like I had finally arrived at the place I was meant to be. This moment of embracing my authenticity came at a young age, shortly after I graduated from high school and decided I wanted to attend college.

I was the first person in my immediate family to pursue a higher education. Choosing a different path than everyone else in my family wasn't easy. I was about to embark on something that no one around me had done, which brought a lot of uncertainty and fear. I still vividly remember the moment I told my mom about my choice to go to college.

You need to understand that in the 1990s, few Latin teenagers discussed attending college with their families. For many, it wasn't even an option due to their family's circumstances. Some couldn't attend because their families needed them to work, while others were told they weren't smart enough or worthy of pursuing higher education. In our culture and generation, going to college wasn't common—it was almost viewed as unattainable. Many Latinos believed (and were often told) that college wasn't something that their parents could afford, and this belief kept countless young people from pursuing their dreams.

When it was my turn to share my dream with my parents, I had no idea how they would respond. I fully expected them to tell me we couldn't afford it—and they would have been right. My parents worked tirelessly every single day of their lives, yet we still lived paycheck to paycheck. That was simply our reality.

But here's the thing—I didn't just want to go to college; I wanted to attend a Christian college and live on campus. I sought the full experience, even though I knew it would be much more expensive than attending a local community college. From a young age, I always wanted to do something different, or as Jamie Kern Lima puts it, "not different, just first."

I aimed to be the first in my family to graduate from college, earn a degree, and attain educational success. I wanted to be the first to secure a stable income and escape living paycheck to paycheck. I sought to be the first to break generational curses. To achieve this, I had to approach things differently. I needed to step outside of what was familiar to experience life in a completely new way.

What's crazy is that in my mind, I thought my parents would expect me to stay home, find a job in the neighborhood, and help until I got married and started my own family. That was the "norm" for everyone I knew—friends, relatives, neighbors. Most of us followed this path, and there was absolutely nothing wrong with it. But I didn't want that for myself. I didn't want to live the norm; I wanted more for myself and for my future. *I wanted to be different; I wanted to be first.*

The idea of having this conversation with my parents as a teenager made me feel afraid and uncertain. My mind raced with questions:

* Will I be able to do this by myself?
* Will I be able to support myself financially?
* Will I be successful?
* Will I make new friends and meet new people?
* Will I make it?

These questions overwhelmed me whenever I thought about going to college. On top of that, there were the extra fears that arose when I considered telling my parents:

* Would they give me their approval?

* Could they assist me financially? (I already knew the answer was no, yet it lingered in my mind.)
* Would they offer support?
* Would they be upset if I wanted to leave home and dorm at the college?

Countless uncertainties weighed heavily on me. But to be honest, I prayed. I prayed fervently, asking God to lead me and guide me on what to say, when to say it, and how to say it.

At that time, not many teenagers rushed to their parents to say they were ready for college, so I truly had no idea what to expect. I even feared my mom might get upset at the thought of me leaving home. As I mentioned earlier, this wasn't the norm for a Latino family. But to be fair to my family, they've always known that I've never been considered "normal."

To my surprise, my parents were proud of me. They were proud that I wanted to go to college and that I chose to do something different. They were so supportive that they couldn't stop telling everyone about my plans to attend college. They were excited and thrilled, and I could feel just how proud they were of me.

I was proud of myself, too. Taking that step to do something completely different from those around us was a monumental moment for me. It turned out to be easier than I expected, and it became my first real experience of freedom, peace, and understanding of what genuine love and support from others truly feel like.

On the day I left for college, my emotions were all over the place. I thought I'd feel only excitement and joy about starting this new chapter—and deep down, I did—but my heart also ached. I was leaving behind everything I knew to be real and familiar to step into something completely new.

I realized I wasn't just leaving my home; I was leaving an old version of myself to start creating a new one. That thought was both thrilling and terrifying. I had no one to hold my hand, no family nearby, and no familiar faces to comfort me. But I knew this was the beginning of something extraordinary—one of the best decisions I would ever make.

It was during my college journey that I discovered the woman I wanted to become, the woman God intended me to be. In those quiet moments, sometimes lonely nights, and on days spent surrounded by friends or studying hard on my own for my psychology, sociology, and business classes, I began to shape my identity. Through the various activities I participated in and the challenges I faced, I gained clarity on who I was and who I aspired to be.

Choosing to become the person you are meant to be—the best version of yourself—won't always be easy. There will be times when you won't have anyone to hold your hand, no family nearby, and no familiar faces to comfort you. You may encounter challenges that leave you questioning, "Did I make the right decision?" Becoming the person, you aspire to be is not for the faint of heart. It requires strength, focus, dedication, faith, and prayer. There will be times when it feels lonely and frightening, but if it's your dream—if you know deep down that you were meant for more—you must never give up.

In those moments, pray harder. Seek guidance from your higher power to help you rise above your emotions and concentrate on what you must do to **'BE YOU'**.

We must learn to step away from the emotional roller coaster that tries to hold us back. To live the life we desire, we can't allow fleeting feelings to dictate our decisions or derail our progress. Stay committed to your path and trust that the effort is worthwhile— because the life you're meant to live is waiting for you on the other side.

Through my experience of doing things differently, I've realized that people are drawn to authenticity. Deep down, everyone craves genuine connections and honesty from others. Think about it—don't you want authenticity in your relationships? If you're reading this book and I'm writing it, and we both value authenticity, that's already two for two.

When I embraced my true self, my circle of friends changed. My new, authentic group of friends understood and accepted me for who I am. They no longer tried to push me to be more like them or pressure me into doing what they wanted. Instead, they respected my values and beliefs. It was liberating to be surrounded by people who valued me for who I am, without expecting me to compromise my identity.

One of the most profound examples of how people responded to my choice to be different occurred during my Christian journey. For a considerable time, I didn't live, speak, behave, or dress like a typical Christian (if such a thing even existed). I immersed myself in the secular world and embraced a secular lifestyle.

Yes, I always believed in God and knew He was with me, but I didn't prioritize Him. My language was rough—I cursed like a truck driver. When I went clubbing, my outfits screamed, "hoochie mama." I could outdrink almost anyone but never let myself get drunk—I was a New Yorker, after all, and always had to stay alert and guarded. The Bible wasn't part of my daily life then. When I eventually decided to truly follow God's Word—or as some say, "come back to Jesus"—it wasn't due to tragedy or trauma. There was no heartbreak, depression, or earth-shattering moment that pushed me to change. My life was relatively normal, yet something felt off. I wasn't satisfied with mere existence; I felt there was more for me, a purpose I wasn't fulfilling.

Have you ever felt that way? Like something was missing, even though everything seemed fine on the surface. That's exactly how I felt. I wasn't having fun anymore; life felt empty. I was tired—tired of merely existing. You've probably heard the phrase "sick and tired of being sick and tired," that's precisely where I was. I wanted more from life. I wanted to do more for others, to be an example, to make a difference. I wanted to be a blessing and help others realize they weren't alone. I wanted to make an impact, to change the world in some way. I didn't know how I was going to do it, but my heart was drawn toward empowering and supporting women. That desire became my guiding force, and it all began with the simple decision to live authentically and align my life with God's purpose.

While I was in college, I seemed to have everything: a supposedly loving fiancé, a great circle of friends, a beautiful apartment, and financial independence with a steady income. Yet, despite what appeared to be a good life, I felt lost and unhappy. There was a persistent emptiness as if I wasn't living my purpose or doing what I was truly meant to do in this world. I had no idea what that purpose was, but I was determined to discover it.

When nothing else seemed to fill that void, I decided to turn to God. I began talking to Him daily, seeking His guidance and direction. Little by little, as I drew closer to Him, things started to make sense. Over the years, through prayer, growth, and studying His Word, my life began to change. The world around me started to feel brighter, more vivid, and undeniably beautiful.

As I read the Word of God, I delved deep within myself and discovered who I truly am. I allowed myself to embrace the authentic person God created me to be. Through this profound journey of self-discovery, I realized my purpose: to help other women uncover their true selves and empower them to reach their full potential.

God began shaping me for this mission, leading me to connect with more women and teaching me how to coach them. I engaged with women through my "Sip with Sidrid" live Facebook videos and met even more during my online boutique sales. These experiences formed the foundation of my coaching journey.

When I shared my new path with others, not everyone understood or supported my decision. Some friends and even family members distanced themselves when I mentioned that I was drawing closer to God and being led to start my own coaching business.

"Coaching? What is that?"

"Is that even a real job?"

"Why would you coach women? What type of coaching are you referring to?

"Is coaching going to make you money?"

"You should stick to what you know, Sidrid."

The criticism was unrelenting. While some of it came from strangers, a significant portion originated from those I cared about. Despite holding degrees in psychology, people questioned my ability to succeed as a coach. Some even suggested that I hadn't reached my full potential, so how could I help others achieve theirs? Ouch that one hurt.

I'll never forget receiving a message from a stranger on social media. She told me I would never succeed, that nobody wanted to hear about God, and that a satanic spell had been cast on me to prevent my vision from coming to life. She vividly described everything she claimed would happen if I continued my pursuit of becoming a Christian Life and Business Transformational Mindset Coach. Even some people I once considered "friends" chose to walk away. They didn't believe in my vision or understand my purpose, and they decided they no longer wished to be part of my life.

If I'm being honest with you (and I always will be #bereal), there were many nights when I cried myself to sleep. I was hurt and confused, unable to understand why some people didn't want me to be my authentic self. Why didn't they want me to be myself? Why didn't they support my desire to help other women experience and learn more about God? It was disappointing, especially because some of these people were my "friends," so I thought.

Through this process, I realized that my authenticity made them uncomfortable because they weren't being genuine with me, or, even worse, with themselves. They weren't true friends. Perhaps they were around because they wanted something from me, or maybe they just wanted to be part of the fun and vibrant community we were creating. But when I chose to grow and change, they didn't want to witness the transformation. They didn't embrace change, which was their choice, not mine.

I once read a quote by Lynn Cowell that said, "Our love for God should be stronger than our fear of humans." That stuck with me. As I grew in the understanding of God's Word, I discovered that to love others genuinely, we must first love ourselves, and loving ourselves means embracing our true selves. It also means releasing the weight of outside opinions and choosing peace over people-pleasing. If you've found joy in who you're becoming, embrace it fully and unapologetically. Walk in your truth. Own your light. You don't owe anyone an explanation for your growth. It's not my job to judge anyone—God didn't give me that assignment, nor did He give anyone that assignment. However, I've noticed that this world spends far too much time worrying about what others think. Which leads me to ask, "Why is that so important?"

I'm not here to criticize social media. I believe it can be a powerful tool, depending on how we choose to use it. Some people use it for good, for business, to support causes, or even to find love. However, others use it to intimidate, harass, insult, and even destroy lives. So here's the real question: Why do we let other people's opinions hinder our thoughts and control our lives and emotions? Why do we give so much power and emotional energy to people we don't know or even those we know who only support us because it's convenient for them? Why do we entertain negativity, drama, and nonsense? Doesn't that sound ridiculous when you think about it?

Ultimately, the only opinions that should truly matter are yours and God's. If you're happy and fulfilling your purpose, don't let anyone dim your light.

I reached a point in my life where it no longer mattered if people chose to step out of my authenticity. Throughout life's journey I learned to recognize and embrace my values, beliefs, and worth. In doing so, the cynical, negative, and uninformed comments from others could no longer penetrate my heart, spirit, or soul. When you realize your true value, beliefs, and worth, you start to see the BEYOUtiful person God created you to be. You see you, you see His masterpiece in you, perfectly crafted and uniquely designed for a purpose.

CHAPTER 11

Accept The New BEYOUtiful You

"The moment you accept yourself you become Beautiful."

~ Rajneesh AKA Osho ~

I once read that BEYOUtiful is simply reality perceived through the eyes of love. As the saying goes, "Beauty is in the eye of the beholder." But let me ask you this: Do you see the beauty in you? Because you are the beholder.

Do you really love yourself?

To become truly authentic with yourself and those around you, you must embrace who you are. You must BE YOU—and recognize the BEYOUty within yourself.

At the very first women's empowerment retreat I facilitated we did an exercise called "Who Am I?" The exercise invited the participants to take a moment for introspection. Each woman moved to a private area with a mirror I provided. Their task was simple yet powerful: to look at themselves in the mirror and write down everything they saw—everything.

I encourage you to do the same.

Here's how it works:

1. Take a piece of paper and a pen.
2. Set a timer—Alexa works well—for 2 minutes.
3. Stand before a mirror and concentrate on your reflection.
4. Describe what you observe—but here's the twist: you must avoid using nouns (such as mom, daughter, business owner, teacher, etc.). Instead, portray yourself with adjectives (like beautiful, proud, lonely, sad, strong, etc.).

Your Task:
Spend the full 2 minutes observing yourself. When the timer goes off, turn to the next page of this book and write down everything you saw in the mirror of yourself. Be honest with yourself. Acknowledge the good, the bad, and even the uncomfortable truths. This exercise is your moment of raw self-reflection, so don't hold back.

What did you see in the mirror?

Loving yourself starts with genuinely knowing who you are. It involves accepting yourself, flaws and all, as the person you were meant to be. As Chapter 7 discusses, knowing who you are entails understanding the unique "ingredients" that make you who you *are*.

Some of those ingredients—such as feelings of depression, sadness, loneliness, or negative self-perceptions—might reflect at you in the mirror. These are the aspects of yourself that you'll need to view differently, to reframe, so you can embrace and love the authentic person you are meant to be. You might ask yourself, "How do I start accepting and embracing the new BEYOUtiful me? Are there steps, a process, or something specific I need to do to help me embrace and celebrate this transformation? Absolutely! The beautiful part is that it begins with something simple yet transformational: BE YOU."

B - **Believing in Yourself.** Accepting the new BEYOUtiful, you start with having confidence in yourself. This is something we all need to work on every day because there will always be negative voices—both external and internal—trying to bring us down. The critics of the world will attempt to shake your confidence, but often, it's the labels we place on ourselves that cause the most harm. When you label yourself with flaws, you start to believe they define you.

But here's the truth: no one in this world is perfect—
we all have imperfections because we're human.
Yet, every one of us, regardless of our backgrounds,
possesses incredible attributes—skills, talents, gifts,
strengths, and abilities. Some of these are innate,
while our life experiences shape others. Unfortunately,
we often hide these remarkable aspects of ourselves,
tucking them away instead of embracing them.

Believing in yourself and in the desires of your heart
is the first step toward recognizing and accepting the
BEYOUty within you. You, along with God, are the only
one who can truly see your unique greatness. While
some people may acknowledge your BEYOUty and
others may not, that should never matter. What truly
counts is how you perceive yourself when you look in
the mirror. If there's something you see in that mirror
that you don't like, it's up to you to change it because
only you can!

We were all created with greatness, but your greatness
is unique—different from mine and everyone else's.
God made you to be entirely one of a kind. Not
even identical twins have the same fingerprints!
The so-called "flaws" you have may actually be life
experiences intentionally designed to mold you into
the person God intended you to be.

These experiences aren't merely lessons—they
are opportunities for growth, to gain wisdom, and

perhaps, one day, to guide others on their journey toward their authentic selves. Remember, your imperfections don't lessen your greatness; they are part of the BEYOUtiful masterpiece God created you to be.

E - **Empower Yourself Daily.** I once heard a powerful statement from motivational speaker Tony Robbins: "Energy is power, and energy is everything." This resonated deeply with me because cultivating energy within us each day is essential for self-empowerment. Maintaining a positive mindset is a critical part of embracing the new BEYOUtiful you.

Elevating your energy allows you to concentrate on self-empowerment through positive affirmations, meditation, power walks, balanced meals, and staying hydrated, to name a few. To truly empower yourself, you must eliminate negative beliefs—those things you speak or think about yourself—and transform them into affirmations that uplift and inspire. You must become your own biggest cheerleader. After all, you are the person who will love yourself the most.

A positive mindset can enhance physical, mental, social, emotional, and spiritual well-being. How you perceive yourself shapes how you feel about yourself and, in turn, how you engage with others. When you empower yourself each day, you cultivate a love for yourself, and self-love is not selfish. As the saying goes, "To love oneself is to acquire wisdom." Self-love is the foundation of self-care, and self-care, at its core, is soul care. The key word here is "self," indicating that it starts with you. It's all about YOU. You must love yourself first, and you can begin to do that by empowering yourself daily.

Remember that a positive mindset isn't something you fix permanently—it's a journey. We're constantly growing and changing, so we must regularly develop a healthier and more accurate view of ourselves. This might involve life coaching, daily affirmations, reading God's word, listening to motivational podcasts (Sip with Sidrid is one of my favorites), or consistently challenging the distorted thoughts we sometimes see in the mirror.

To start shifting your mindset, you must first decide that you want to change. It begins with a choice. Here are some affirmations you can say to yourself while looking in the mirror. Speak them out loud, just like I do. Are you ready?

Come on, let's do it together...

I AM... STRONG
I AM... HEARD
I AM... ENOUGH
I AM... INSPIRED
I AM... SPECTACULAR

I AM... MAGNIFICENT

I AM... EMPOWERED

I AM... BLESSED

I AM... LOVED

I AM... POWERFUL

I AM... WISE

I AM... SPECIAL

I AM... GODS CHOSEN

I AM... TREASURED

I AM... CREATED FOR A PURPOSE

I AM... CAPABLE

I AM... PROSPEROUS

I AM... ACCEPTED

I AM... SUCCESSFUL

I AM... WORTHY

I AM... A CHILD OF GOD

I AM... UNIQUE

I AM... PROTECTED

I AM... BEAUTIFUL

I AM... FEARLESS

I AM... IMPORTANT

I AM... SMART

I AM... WEALTHY

I AM... HEALTHY

I AM... WONDERFULLY MADE

I AM... THE DAUGHTER OF THE KING OF KINGS

I AM... A MASTERPIECE

Y – **YOU ARE A MASTERPIECE.** This is one of the

most powerful affirmations you can live by because it's backed by biblical truth: You are God's masterpiece. Through my faith, I know that I am royalty—I am a daughter of the King of Kings. Think about that for a moment. Return to the mirror and truly see yourself as royalty. Recognize yourself as a daughter or son of the King of Kings, a chosen child, someone He absolutely loves. View yourself as someone created in His image, endowed with gifts of limitless grace, mercy, and love.

How does that make you feel? Empowered? Loved? Valued? Accepted? Worthy? Joyful?

I frequently reflect on my heavenly Father, and because of my faith in Him, I understand that I am His masterpiece. This truth reminds me that I am worthy of being myself and of becoming the woman I am meant to be, and guess what? So are you.

When I encounter negative thoughts, such as feelings of unworthiness or a lack of self-love (and yes, I still battle them; it's a daily struggle), I remind myself that I am God's masterpiece. Since I was created authentically in His image, I can truly embrace the new BEYOUtiful me.

Here's an exercise you can incorporate into your daily routine:

* *Position yourself in front of a mirror.*

* *Look at yourself and discover the royalty within you.*
* *Imagine yourself as the daughter or son of the King of Kings, the chosen child, deeply loved and uniquely crafted in His image.*
* *Put on a crown if you need to, and see God's Princess, God's Prince.*
* *Reflect on the gifts you have received—grace, mercy, and unconditional love.*

Take a moment to appreciate how that makes you feel. Allow yourself to feel empowered, grateful, and at peace. Breathe in that sensation, let it settle in your soul, and exhale gratitude, knowing that you are blessed, uniquely created, and fearfully and wonderfully made.

That, my friend, is the true essence of BEYOUty.

O - **OPEN YOUR HEART.** Embrace new possibilities and celebrate the BEYOUtiful you. Learn to love yourself and appreciate the life you're creating. Allow yourself to listen more closely to your inner voice and fully believe in yourself. Open your heart to the things that bring you joy and intentionally focus on them, for your happiness will flourish when you prioritize what truly makes you happy. Happiness begins from within—it's a gift only you can give yourself. Open your heart to recognize the BEYOUty within you and the greatness God has created in you.

Opening your heart is a deliberate and purposeful action, essential for nurturing your authenticity. When you truly know and embrace who you are, it unlocks your potential, propels your growth, and allows you to fully become the BEYOUtiful person you were always meant to be.

U – **UNLEASH THE NEW BEYOUtiful YOU.** You are ready to fully embrace and become the person you've been striving to become. Don't hold yourself back from being your true self. You've worked hard to become the traveler, photographer, teacher, best friend, wife, mother, incredible employee, business owner, entrepreneur, artist, philanthropist, survivor, doctor, educator, coach, stay-at-home mom, lover, or simply the authentic person God created you to be. You've unearthed your authenticity after years of burying it—perhaps to help others or to hide parts of yourself that they weren't ready to see. But today is the day to unleash the amazing person within you. Embrace your greatness. Share your flaws and scars with the world, for they have shaped you into the incredible person you are today.

Sometimes, when I look in the mirror, my mind tries to replay images of who I used to be and the things I used to do. Those limiting beliefs occasionally sneak in and whisper: "You're still fat. You're still ugly. No one cares about you. No one believes in what you're saying. You're not helping anyone. So many people hate you." However, as I mentioned earlier, self-love and our self-perception in the mirror are not permanently fixed. It's a journey. We must continuously work to cultivate a healthier and more accurate view of ourselves, replacing those distorted reflections with the truth of who we are.

Today, things are different. When those limiting thoughts arise in me—and in you—we must choose to change the narrative. We must remind ourselves to simply **'BE YOU'**. **B**elieve in yourself. **E**mpower yourself through affirmations, meditations, the Word of God, and inspirational books. Remind yourself that **Y**ou are God's masterpiece. **O**pen your heart to new and amazing possibilities. **U**nleash the **BEYOU**ty within—the **BEYOU**ty that God uniquely created in you.

Now, when we look in the mirror, we can see beyond the lies. We recognize God's greatness within us. We understand that we deserve love, respect, abundance, peace, joy, happiness, self-love, self-care, fulfillment, and freedom.

Will you encounter challenges? Absolutely. But you must remain true to your authenticity and the amazing person you're becoming—you will shine through.

I'll never forget the day I received a call from an up-line leader during my time in direct selling. She had scheduled a coaching call with me, and during our conversation, she told me that I wasn't a "team player." I was stunned by this comment. I attended every meeting, consistently met my sales goals, regularly asked questions, and earned a great income. My success directly benefited her, as she earned a substantial commission from my sales as one of her downline consultant.

I asked her, "Why do you think I'm not a team player?" Her response shocked me: it was because I didn't comply with her personal requirements for consultants on her team—requirements that made no sense. These rules had nothing to do with helping us increase sales, advance within the company, or build stronger teams. Instead, they seemed to serve her personal agenda, creating the illusion of a unified team that conformed to her specific desires and preferences.

At first, I thought she was joking I even laughed. But when I asked, "Are you serious?" she replied, "Yes." Here I was, being coached by a six-figure income earner, who was supposed to help me grow my business, build my team, and achieve success. As uncomfortable as her demands felt—and as silly as I thought they were—I complied. After all, I wanted to be a "team player," and I, too, aspired to earn a six-figure income.

After I complied for about two months, I felt uncomfortable; it seemed as if I was being pressured to do and be someone I wasn't. Her request just wasn't me. It was so far from my authenticity that I couldn't take myself seriously, let alone expect others to. When I told her I wouldn't comply with her personal requirements any longer because it wasn't who I was and had no relevance to increasing my sales, sponsorships, or leadership, she snapped. She told me I was "Un-coachable," and that she wasn't going to waste her time with me.

Just like that, she decided she wouldn't coach me anymore. Not because I wasn't committed to my business, but because I didn't conform to her personal, self-imposed rules—rules that had nothing to do with actual business growth. Her expectations weren't about helping her team succeed; they were about showcasing her influence and control. If anyone wanted to do things their way, she didn't consider them "part of the team."

That experience taught me a valuable lesson: true leadership isn't about compelling others to follow your vision but enabling them to flourish in their own authenticity.

That's when it hit me—she didn't want consultants to grow their businesses; she wanted followers. Her requests had nothing to do with actual success or building a business. For a moment, I felt upset and angry, but then I realized the truth: she wanted people to do whatever she asked of without any question. That didn't sit well with me, so I decided to forge my own path.

Rather than conforming, I sought out other successful six-figure income earners and studied their strategies. I gained insights from their teachings, coaching, and examples. I attended conventions, training sessions, and zoom meetings. I built connections with other inspiring, high-achieving leaders in the company. I concentrated on growing my business, increasing sales, and quickly assembling a large thriving team. With hard work and dedication, I earned recognition, awards, and prizes—including all-expenses-paid vacations. Most importantly, I proved to myself, and to those who doubted me, that I was coachable, capable, and successful; and in under two years, I accomplished what many believed was impossible: I ranked among the top 1% of income earners in the company and received the esteemed Elite Leader title.

I share this with you because it's essential to create the life you want to see—both in the mirror and in the world around you. If there's something in the mirror you don't like, change it. Only you can. There will always be people who want you to follow their path, convincing you that their way is what is best for you when in reality, it's only best for them. They might try to tell you that your way is wrong, that your feelings are invalid, or even that your goals, dreams, and ambitions do not align with God's purpose for your life. Some will doubt you and insist that your dreams are not worth pursuing and that you will never achieve them. However deep down inside, you know that's not true. Listen to that instinct. Trust the nudge placed in your heart or in the pit of your stomach—it will always lead and guide you in the right direction.

It doesn't matter if being true to yourself makes you feel different from everyone else; being different is a gift. In a world where so many people strive to blend in, standing out is remarkable. As Jamie Kern Lima puts it, being "first" or different (in my words) means stepping beyond the comfortable, breaking free from limitations, and daring to explore new ground. Being different isn't always easy—it can be challenging and sometimes lonely. However, it's never a bad thing. Being different is what makes you unique. It's your authenticity. It means living your life on your own terms, grounded in your values and beliefs. For some, being different can make you appear adventurous, interesting, or even inspiring. It signifies a willingness to experiment with life, embrace your uniqueness, your authenticity. It allows you to unapologetically **'BE YOU'**.

Celebrate your differences. Embrace your authenticity, it's what makes you BEYOUtiful.

CHAPTER 12

Praise & Celebrate The New BeYoutiful You!

"The more you praise and celebrate your life, the more there is in life to celebrate."

~ Oprah Winfrey ~

By now, you should have realized that it's not about changing yourself—it's about discovering yourself and allowing your true self to shine through. Once you've decided to show others the amazing person you are, it's time to celebrate you—the BEYOUtiful individual you've become.

Take a moment to thank God, the universe, or whoever you believe is your higher power. You've achieved a realization, a goal, a destination that many people in this world may never attain—or even recognize as absent from their lives. You took the time to acknowledge your unhappiness, to realize that you weren't living the life you truly desired, and you chose to change it. You decided to make a difference for yourself and, if I may be honest, for everyone who crosses your path. By embracing your authenticity, you inspire others to do the same.

Celebrate the fact that you invested in yourself, that you realized you matter, and that you are worthy of being exactly who you were created to be. Celebrate that you found the real you and that you had the courage to embrace the new you. Celebrate that you are learning to love yourself, that you are discovering what you want in life and celebrate that you now refuse to let others disrespect or define you.

Celebrate that you know you have a voice and that your voice is worth hearing. Celebrate that you are BEYOUtiful—inside and out. You are amazing, intelligent, valuable, loved, and worthy. You are the child of the King of Kings, God's masterpiece, and the author of your own story.

Even on days when your mind tries to derail you with self-doubt, you've learned how to overcome that "stinking thinking" and remain true to yourself. As Tiny Buddha wisely states, *"You deserve to celebrate not only who you've become, but who you could have become— and fought not to be."*

Step into your power each day. Celebrate yourself for the amazing, unique individual God created in you, and live a life that reflects your authenticity, your worth, and your purpose.

> "Today you are you,
> that is truer than true.
> There is no one alive
> who is more You then You."
>
> ~ Dr. Seuss ~

> "Praise and Celebrate the new
> BEYOUtiful you.
> Praise and Celebrate
> because you now know
> to BE YOU."
>
> ~ Sidrid Rivera ~

Discovering your authenticity is a gift—not everyone can experience or embrace it. Now that you've embarked on this journey, we share the responsibility to help others uncover what we have learned and the peace that comes with truly knowing and accepting ourselves. God calls us to be a blessing to others, and we should strive to guide and inspire those around us. Assist them in uncovering the desires of their hearts, achieving their goals, and recognizing their own unique beauty and authenticity—just as you have through the exercises and reflections in this book. Be proud of yourself and let your transformation be seen. Be an example by simply being the new BEYOUtiful you. Let others see the confidence you've discovered within yourself, the love you've cultivated for who you are, and the worth you now embrace. Speak about yourself with respect, radiate your newfound self-belief, and demonstrate how you've grown from hiding like a caterpillar to soaring as a butterfly. Let the world see the BEYOUty that God always intended for you to be.

When people—whether skeptics, secret believers, or proud supporters—ask you how you accomplished this, bless them with a copy of this book. I know it may sound strange coming from me as the author, but if this book has influenced you, think about how much it could help someone else. Pass on the blessing. Sharing this book is like recommending your favorite restaurant, a new dessert you adore, or a movie that inspired you. When something resonates with you deeply, you naturally want to share it.

I wrote this book as a resource to inspire, empower, and guide everyone. If it has been life-changing, encouraging, thought-provoking, or even surprising for you, please pass it on so that others can experience the same transformation. Remember that the journey of self-discovery and authenticity is a lifelong adventure. Every step you take toward personal growth, self-awareness, and empowerment brings you closer to your true potential and the life you genuinely desire. Stay committed to your journey. Celebrate your successes, learn from your setbacks, and never stop empowering yourself to live authentically. Pursue a life that aligns with your deepest values and aspirations, knowing that your potential is limitless and your journey uniquely yours.

Remember, the habits and patterns you form today will shape who you become tomorrow. Focus on creating a balanced and fulfilling life by prioritizing your well-being—don't let what happened to me happen to you; the world doesn't need more diabetics! Take care of yourself, seek clarity in your vision, and embrace the tools shared in this book to stay motivated and persevere, even when the road gets tough.

It's Time to BEYOUtify Your Life.

As you close this final chapter, I want to leave you with one powerful truth: it's not just about who you are on the inside—it's also about the environment that surrounds you every day. Now that you've done the soul work, it's time to BEYOUtify your home, your workplace, and your life.

Why? Because the spaces you occupy should support your growth, reflect your truth, and empower you to remain connected to the person God created you to be. What surrounds you has the power to elevate you—or hold you back. And you deserve to be uplifted every day.

Activate your five senses and explore how to intentionally BEYOUtify every area of your life:

● **Sight** – What you see impacts how you feel. Decorate with items that inspire joy and peace: fresh flowers, inspirational quotes, or even butterflies—symbols of transformation. Use vibrant colors that awaken your spirit. Even your wardrobe matters! Start adding pops of color to your closet—no more hiding in black or gray unless you intentionally choose it.

🜚 **Smell** – Scents carry memory and emotion. Fill your home or office with fragrances that calm and center you—such as lavender for peace or citrus for energy. Allow the air around you to infuse your day with vitality.

♩ **Sound** – Play music that resonates with your soul. Whether it's worship, affirmations, jazz, or nature sounds, allow what you listen to uplift your spirit. Silence the noise of the world and focus on what makes your heart beat strong.

👣 **Touch** – Surround yourself with textures that make you feel safe, warm, and comforted. A cozy blanket, a soft sweater, or a velvet cushion may seem small, but they remind you that you are worthy of care.

🐱 **Taste** – Nourish yourself in ways that energize both your body and soul. Light a candle and enjoy a cup of herbal tea or a glass of wine. Sit down and savor your food instead of rushing through your meals. Your body is your temple—feed it with love.

When your surroundings align with your identity, something powerful happens—you live in your truth, not just talk about it. You start attracting more peace, joy, and abundance because you've made space for it. Every detail becomes a reflection of your wholeness.

So go ahead, my friend. BEYOUtify your world. Let your surroundings remind you daily of who you are and whose you belong to.

You made it to the end of this book—but this is just the beginning of your breakthrough.

You've read the words, reflected on the truth, and hopefully challenged the lies that once held you back. Now it's time to take action. Don't just close this book—open your life to the freedom, purpose, and confidence that's been waiting for you all along.

You are not alone in this journey. As long as I'm alive, you have a sister cheering you on. I see you, I believe in you, and I love you—because I am you. I've walked through the fire, faced the doubts, and found the power that comes when a woman decides to rise and become the version of herself that God always intended her to be. So now it's your turn.

You are God's masterpiece—created with intention, covered in grace, designed by the almighty, chosen with love, and destined for greatness.

Believe it. Own it. Walk boldly in it.

And when you're ready for more, I'll be here—walking this journey with you. Look for us and visit us to discover where we're headed to next. We'll be taking the "BE YOU Movement" on the road with powerful, state-to-state Women's Empowerment Summits, and conducting our yearly retreats. Come and join us, I'd love to hug you in person, hear your story, and celebrate the woman you're becoming.

You've done enough surviving. Now it's time to be seen, to be strong, and to **BE YOU!**

I love you even though I may not know you.

Choose to always live happy and blessed.

Sidrid Rivera

Appendix: Frequently Asked Questions (F&A)

1. What inspired you to write BE YOU?
I wrote BE YOU from a deeply personal place of healing, growth, and faith. I wanted to create a guide for women who are tired of performing, hiding, or doubting themselves. This book is a call to rise into the woman God created you to be—authentically, boldly, and without apology.

2. Is this book only for women of faith?
While BE YOU is rooted in biblical principles and my Christian faith, the message is universal. Any woman who's ready to rediscover her worth, silence her inner critic, and walk in purpose will benefit from this journey.

3. Can the author coach people who live outside of her state?
Absolutely! My coaching programs are available to women nationwide—and internationally. I work virtually via Zoom, so no matter where you live, we can connect.

4. How can I schedule a coaching session or consultation with the author?
You can schedule a free consultation with me directly

through my website. Visit: https://sidridrivera.com/business-life/ola/services/free-consultation

5. What types of coaching programs do you offer?
I offer various coaching options including one-on-one coaching, group sessions, spiritual and mindset coaching, and business development programs. Each one is designed to meet you where you are and walk with you as you grow into who you're meant to be.

6. Do I need to read the book before starting coaching?
No, but it's highly recommended. BE YOU lays the foundation for the mindset and heart posture we'll build on in coaching. Many of my clients read the book and then schedule a session to go deeper.

7. What is the main message of BE YOU?
That your identity is not defined by the world, your past, or your pain. You were created with divine intention, and your worth doesn't require validation. It's time to release fear, embrace freedom, and walk boldly as YOU.

8. Will there be a workbook or companion journal to go with the book?
Yes! I'm currently working on a BE YOU Daily Declaration Journal and other resources to help you implement the teachings from the book into your

daily life. In addition, this book has already started your healing journey with the exercises and tasks implemented into this book.

9. Can this book be used in a women's group or book club?
Absolutely. In fact, BE YOU is perfect for group discussion. I've also created discussion questions and coaching prompts for each chapter to help guide group sessions or individual reflections. You can get the guide and discussion questions by visiting https://sidridrivera.com/resources.

10. Are speaking engagements or book signings available?
Yes, I am available for speaking engagements, conferences, women's events, and book signings. For booking information, please visit my website or email sidrid@sidridrivera.com.

11. What makes your coaching different from others?
My coaching is Spirit-led, faith-based, and deeply transformational. With over 20 years of experience in mindset, life, and business coaching, I combine biblical truths, practical tools, and deep empathy to help women unlock the version of themselves that God already sees.

12. How do I stay connected with you and your movement?

You can follow me on all social platforms via https://linktr.ee/SidridRiveraEnterprises and join the BE YOU Movement email list for updates on events, resources, and special offers.

13. Is BE YOU suitable for teenagers or young adults?
Yes, the content is appropriate and empowering for older teens and young adults, especially those struggling with identity, confidence, and self-worth. It can be a powerful resource for mothers and daughters to read together.

14. Will there be future books in the BE YOU series?
Yes! The BE YOU movement is just getting started. Stay tuned for companion devotionals, affirmation decks, journals, and new book projects to continue supporting your growth.

15. What should I do after finishing the book?
Reflect, pray, and take action. Then visit https://sidridrivera.com to explore women empowerment retreats, business and personal growth summits, coaching options or download free resources to support your next step. And most importantly—share it with someone who needs the reminder that it's okay to **BE YOU.**

Sidrid Rivera

Sidrid Rivera knows what it's like to feel unworthy, lost in self-doubt, depression, and loneliness. But she also knows what it means to rise. As a woman who has overcome deep personal battles, Sidrid is living proof that transformation is possible. Today, she empowers others to do the same—as a motivational speaker, author, and CEO of Sidrid Rivera Enterprises, a faith-based life and business transformational mindset coaching company. With over 23 years of coaching experience, she helps women step boldly into their authenticity, confidence, and God-given purpose.

Armed with degrees in Psychology, Sociology, and Business, Sidrid blends her academic insight with real-life experience to guide women toward lasting change. She is the host of the "Sip w/ Sidrid" Podcast and is committed to helping others align their success with their faith. Married for 23 years and dog mom to three lovable Labradors, Sidrid finds fulfillment in faith, family, and serving women ready to break free from limitations and live the life they were created for.

Stay Connected, Be Blessed.

If BE YOU spoke to your heart, imagine what's possible when we meet face-to-face and grow together in a room full of powerful, purpose-driven women. That's why in 2026, we're taking the BE YOU Movement on the road with state-by-state Women's Empowerment Summits designed to help you embrace your authenticity, unlock your purpose, and walk boldly in your God-given identity. I'd love to hug you in person, hear your story, and celebrate the woman you're becoming.

Let's stay connected — your breakthrough is only just beginning.

🔗 Stay in the Loop: Scan the QR Code below or visit:

🌐 Website: www.sidridrivera.com

📘 Facebook: Sidrid Rivera Enterprises

📷 Instagram: @sidridriveraenterprises

🎵 TikTok: @sidridriveraenterprises

💬 Let's Hear From You! - Leave a Review of 'BE YOU' on Amazon or your favorite platform! Your story may inspire another woman to begin hers.

🛍️ Want More? - Shop swag, empowerment workbooks, and event tickets at

🛒 https://creativesoldesigns.net/shop/ols/categories/be-you-book-merch

📓 Coming in 2026 Women's Empowerment Summits - We're coming to a city near you! Check the schedule, reserve your spot and get your ticket early, and bring a friend at https://sidridrivera.com/

🎙️ *Stay connected daily via our Podcast:*

* Spotify Podcast Link: https://bit.ly/3Y5NUcW
* Amazon Podcast Link: https://amzn.to/47SLRfM
* Apple Podcast Link: https://apple.co/3Y3O6JO
* iHeart Radio Podcast Link: https://www.iheart.com/pod…/269-sip-with-sidrid-271080419/
* Youtube: https://www.youtube.com/@sidridrivera

SRE Facebook:	SRE Instagram:	SRE Website:

SRE LinkTree:	SRE YouTube:	SRE TikTok:

SRE Pinterest:

SRE Podcasts:

Spotify Podcast:	Amazon Podcast:	Apple Podcast:	iHeart Podcast:

www.ingramcontent.com/pod-product-compliance
Lightning Source LLC
Chambersburg PA
CBHW070641160426
43194CB00009B/1534